Letting Nicki Go

A Mother's Journey
through Her Daughter's Cancer

Letting Nicki Go

A Mother's Journey
through Her Daughter's Cancer

Bunny Leach

atmosphere press

To Jesse

TABLE OF CONTENTS

FOREWORD

I first met Bunny Leach through an e-mail she sent me after reading my book, *The Shop on Blossom Street*. One of the characters, Lydia Hoffman, survived brain cancer as a teenager, and, as the story begins, Lydia opens a yarn store in Seattle as an affirmation of life. Fittingly enough, Bunny found my book at a yarn store, one in North Carolina. Because of her daughter, Nicki, she immediately identified with the story and particularly with this character. But Lydia survived two bouts of cancer. Unfortunately, Nicki didn't.

Eventually Bunny joined me at a book signing in Florida, and we connected not only as author and reader but as friends.

The difference between my story and Bunny's is that hers is a story she's lived. In *Letting Nicki Go*, Bunny has shared the beauty of her beloved Nicki's life and the grief caused by her death. Through Nicki's illness, her diagnoses and treatments and then death, Bunny experienced one of the many truths about cancer—that it devastates not only its victims but their survivors. During those painful, difficult years, Bunny also learned to accept that devastation and turned it into something that would benefit others. She's done it through this book and through the Nicki Leach Foundation, a nonprofit organization that helps other young people with cancer. I encourage you to check out her website and, if possible, make a donation.

And, above all, I encourage you to read this book! It will touch your heart and encourage you, as it did me. Bunny claims I inspired her, but the truth is she inspires me. I'm proud to be linked to her and to Nicki's story.

Letting Nicki Go shows us the unfailing love between this mother and daughter, as well as their profound faith, the kind of faith that makes it possible to endure the unendurable. This is a deeply moving, intimate, and ultimately inspiring portrait, a story that will stay with you.

Bunny proves that there's light in even the darkest tragedy—and what greater tragedy is there than the loss of a child? Her telling of Nicki's story will bring courage to anyone facing that same loss. Or any loss at all...

—Debbie Macomber

PROLOGUE

A Time to Be Still

When I walk around my town and go to the grocery store, the post office, or even the bank, I always have to fight back insistent tears. I wish I were invisible. People mean well, but they stare at me. I know what they're thinking: "Look, there's that poor woman whose teenage daughter died from cancer. And isn't it sad that her husband left her too?"

My mind shouts out: *please, stop pitying me! It's too painful.*

I could run away and hide—move away from my town and start over—but where would I go? I can't leave a place where I hold so many happy memories of my daughter's younger days. Even though there are unbearable memories here now, there are good ones too: I still can feel her presence here, still hear her laughter. She had porcelain skin and eyes the color of the sea; her hair was smooth as silk, long and blonde like the color of beach sand, and when she stood barefoot in the water, her hair flowed with the wind. She was always smiling—even while she battled cancer.

Our private beach was our favorite place to relax and talk. We would walk together for miles along the water's edge during the time that she battled cancer. In fact, her last photo was taken on our beloved beach, on Thanksgiving Day. She stood barefoot in the sand, her hair waving softly in the breeze, both thumbs slipped through the belt loops of her blue jeans. She wore a simple white T-shirt and a warm smile. She was content. At the time, I didn't know it would be our last Thanksgiving together. Then, we still had hope that God would grant us a miracle.

Now, I walk alone on this beach, but I still feel her beside me. Because of that, I'm afraid to leave. This is where I watched her grow from a little girl to a beautiful young woman. This is where she honed her skills as an actress—she aspired to one day move to New York City and make her debut on Broadway, but she never got the chance. I can't leave here because I feel her spirit floating on the ocean breeze; I see visions of her splashing in the water, laughing, or on the shore building sand castles. And so, I remain.

They say that while grieving you shouldn't make any substantial decisions or undergo big changes to your life. They say this is a time to be still.

Or at least, so I was told.

LEARNING TO LIVE AGAIN

"Laurie told me he loved you more than me—and I did a terrible thing, Jo! I flew into a rage, ran upstairs to your desk in the attic, and tore your novel to shreds and threw them in the fire!" Nicki exclaimed.

So determined was Nicki to get the role of Amy in the local community theater's production of *Little Women*, she had memorized all of Amy's lines even before her audition. Seventy-eight young hopefuls showed up, vying for the various roles, but when the call came from casting offering Nicki the role, she just smiled confidently, as if to say, "What did you expect, Mom?"

Nicki planned to move from her hometown—the place she grew up, performed in community theater, and studied dance and singing—in order to live out her dream in New York City: the Big Apple. She knew that one day she'd get her big break on Broadway. She could *see* it. She could *taste* it.

Her dreams were like those of a lot of girls her age, especially girls who loved the theater, but she was so good. Whether she was on or off the stage, Nicki's captivating personality sparkled. When Nicki was eight years old, a reporter from the local paper asked her what her future plans were. Nicki replied that she wanted to be in a movie or to act on Broadway "as soon as possible." Acting was in her blood, and I was thrilled that she had a passion for something so early in her life.

But Nicki never got her chance; she never got her big break. Nicki died on April 29, 2005, from a malignant brain tumor, at the age of nineteen. She left the stage bare and her family bereft, but she also left her mother a legacy that taught her not just how to survive, but how to find joy in life once again. It wasn't easy, and it wasn't quick. Switching gears and learning how to go on without her has been hard. The many dreams that I held in my heart for our future together are gone now. My longing to one day applaud her on Broadway, to be the mother of the bride, won't happen for me now. My future has changed, and I must begin to heal. As years continue to pass, I work on putting the pieces of my life back together, while building my future and letting go of past dreams. Slowly, I've started to live again, realizing that constantly going back to the past is not healthy or where my mind should be, as in the end it was devastating watching Nicki suffer. Instead I'm starting to bring forward joyful memories of her, and choosing to let go of the pain. I know that I will see her again, and this is the promise that I carry with me every day.

Sometimes I think about other mothers who have also lost a child, and wonder if they feel what I'm feeling. After Nicki died, I became part of a select group—a secret club— one that I certainly didn't want to be a part of. Nobody *wants* to be a member of the grieving mothers club. But even if I don't choose to attend the meetings now, I'm still a part of the club. I know I would feel understood and not be pitied in these groups—I certainly don't want anyone's pity, but that's what I get at times—because each of us knows personally just how deep the pain goes. Some parents like to meet in groups to talk about their loss, their pain, and their grief: somehow, we seem to sniff each other out, sensing that we're not the only ones suffering the loss of a child, or grieving the loneliness of that special bond we once had. I know how important being together is so we can talk and recognize that we are not alone in our pain. But I'm not ready to do this yet; I don't want to talk about how I feel right now. It's just too painful to face other parents' pain because I haven't completely faced my own yet. It's still too raw. And ultimately anyone who has lost a child can only feel and understand her own personal experience: I want to be alone in my mind with my child. Maybe in time I will, though. I don't know what the future will bring.

Some parents, those who lost a child suddenly, like to remind me of how lucky I am that I was able to say good-bye to my child. But losing a beloved child is a no-win situation. When I think of the horror they were spared by not seeing their child waste away, suffering years of constant physical pain and degradation, I disagree. Watching my daughter suffer, unable to alleviate her pain, was heartbreaking. But then—loss is not a competition. Grieving mothers cannot compare their pain, because we are all equal in our loss. After losing a child, we know that this pain is the most devastating of all, no matter the circumstances. I find it comforting that we don't want to be isolated in our pain, like Nicki was when she went through her treatments—and yet we are.

Losing Nicki changed me. I love deeper than I ever did before; I enjoy solitude and quiet more; I'm not afraid of much anymore, it seems. Anyone who hasn't lost a child couldn't possibly know how this feels. I wouldn't expect you to. Grieving complicates your thinking. I started grieving the day we got Nicki's diagnosis, a glioblastoma, when her pediatric neurosurgeon told us that most people die from the disease within three years. Before the diagnosis I had been praying for a miracle, and now I hoped that God would heal her. But as the years passed and we approached the year-three mark, and all her treatments and surgeries had failed us, I still couldn't give up hope. And when Nicki tried to tell me that she might be losing her battle with cancer, trying to prepare me for the worst, I just kept praying for my miracle. Even near the end, when Nicki wanted my help in getting her affairs in order and even asked my permission to surrender, I wouldn't listen. It would have gone against my convictions, and destroyed my hope that my miracle would surely come. Anything else was unthinkable. It hurt so much to watch her suffer and not be able to save her. Denial was my survival.

Toward the end, she just wanted to relax. She was so tired: she wanted to rest and see her friends, to be at peace before her time ran out; she was asking me to understand that she was exhausted. Instead, I told her "keep fighting," and encouraged her to continue to go for treatments—even when her doctors told us that there were no more options: the treatments weren't working. Nicki was more realistic than I was. *Doctors are not God,* I told myself. They had done all that they could do for her, but I hoped that God would intervene. How couldn't a mother do this?

Five years later, my mind has begun to heal—a little— and I can better see behind me; they say, after all, that hindsight is 20/20. The fog has started to clear, and I realize just how smart, practical, mature, and wise my Nicki really was. I can understand that it was getting harder for her to fight near the end. She was tired but I kept pushing her because I was scared: losing her was more than I could imagine. Nicki knew that I was afraid, and did everything she could to help me survive my pain, even if it meant going against her wishes. I'm not sure when our roles changed, and she became the adult.

Now, as I move forward to embrace the present, choosing to enjoy life one day at a time, I feel my daughter's living spirit. I know she can witness me enjoying each day, and this is why I can smile again. I often look up to the sky and wish on the brightest, most beautiful star shining from heaven—one I now call "Star 17"—and know that Nicki is watching over me. She always loved stars. I remember the day I helped her cover her bedroom ceiling with glow-in-the-dark stars of every shape and color. When we turned the light out, her room looked just like a night sky full of stars. Whenever she wrote her name, she drew a star to dot both *i*'s. Indeed, her dream was always to move to NYC and to become a star on Broadway. I find it symbolic, and a bit mystical, that her tumor was discovered just days before her seventeenth birthday. Could she have somehow known that Star 17 was her fate?

My daughter's spirit is now dancing and singing throughout our universe. I feel her when I see butterflies flutter by my window, or when I see stars twinkle overhead, or—especially—when I hear the song "I Hope You Dance," because that is how I see her now: dancing. She always wanted a red Mini Cooper, and now I see them everywhere—at times they seem to appear out of nowhere, following me! When that happens, I know it's her. I think of these symbols as Nicki's way of letting me know that she will always be watching over me here on earth. Sometimes she speaks to me in my heart, telling me that she misses me, but that she's smiling as well. Whenever I become overwhelmed with missing her, I close my eyes and embrace the sorrow, because I know this sadness will eventually pass. And then I can smile again, something I had stopped doing while she was suffering.

Through her death, Nicki helped me to become a better person; now my mission and purpose in life are to help others who are going through similar situations. I do this through my writing and my work as a patient advocate, as well as by helping other young adults with cancer through Nicki's memorial foundation, the Nicki Leach Foundation. And with time, I plan to help with clinical trials for glioblastoma; if there had been a cure, perhaps she wouldn't have died. Doing these things to help others in turn helps me survive her loss.

Life is very different for me now. Nicki gave me her strength: death doesn't scare me anymore. Even though I still talk to her every day and long to hold her in my arms, I have accepted what I had no control over—her death—and I keep moving forward. I think Nicki would like that. She kept a positive attitude about everything in her life—good or bad—and she was the one who helped me accept her death by witnessing her strength. When I think about her bravery and optimism as she battled cancer, I realize that it was important to her that I be strong and healthy. And I will be now, because I feel that I owe this to her and to myself.

She was my mentor, helping to prepare me to live without her, all the while knowing that I might not get my miracle and she might not survive. Nicki set an example for me with her continued words of hope. "I'm feeling great today, Mommy," she would often tell me, even on day five of her chemo rounds when I knew she must actually be nauseated. She cared about my state of mind, and so she always encouraged me to spend time with my friends, knowing that one day I would need them more than ever.

She didn't want to be a burden, and she never was—I would have spent the rest of my life taking care of her. In the end, she was the one who helped pave my road to acceptance, no matter what the outcome might be. Nicki did not want to live differently, nor did she want me to live differently and let cancer control our lives in any way. That was my Nicki: she was filled with kindness and compassion, even through the years that she battled her disease. When anyone wanted to visit her—even if she wasn't feeling well—she would always welcome them and say yes, because she genuinely cared about others, not just herself.

As I lay in bed beside her on her last morning, my head gently resting against her cheek, she took a deep breath in. I knew it was her last. Her brother Jesse placed his hand softly over her heart as the rapid beating slowed, and then stopped. I kissed her lips, and felt God's grace come over me. He soothed and comforted my soul that sorrowful day.

Nicki died peacefully and beautifully, exiting this earth much like she entered it: quietly, softly, with grace and dignity. And when she took her last breath, I felt her spirit float to Heaven, along with half of my heart: it followed her to God, and will stay there with her until we meet again.

I THOUGHT THIS WAS PARADISE

The city of Ponte Vedra Beach, Florida, has one of the most pristine stretches of beach along the Atlantic Ocean, boasting one of the most extravagant zip codes in the country... but cancer can follow you wherever you go. Whether rich or poor, young or old, black or white, you cannot run or hide from this disease—not even in paradise.

In 1987, my husband Mike retired from the Association of Tennis Professionals men's tour. At this point in our marriage, it was getting hard to travel with our young children—two-year-old Nicki, and our son, four-year-old Jesse—and we wanted to settle down and let the kids have a more stable life than traveling internationally for tournaments. So, Mike accepted a job as tennis director at the Atlanta Health & Racquet Club; and, after five years in Atlanta, he was offered, and ultimately decided to accept, a position as the Director of Tennis at the Ponte Vedra Inn & Club in Florida. At the time, Jesse was nine and Nicki was seven. Both kids would grow up playing tennis on courts that, in 2002, *Tennis* magazine recognized as one of the nation's top fifty tennis facilities. I hoped that this city would be where we could finally settle down as a family. After making three major moves, first from Michigan to Atlanta and then to Florida, and having traveled with our two babies all over the world on Mike's professional tennis tours, all the while living out of suitcases and hotel rooms, I found the nomadic lifestyle to be *challenging*, to say the least. Finally, I thought, we would have a more normal life as a family, and looked forward to raising my children in Florida and supporting my husband in his career.

After working closely with a realtor, I eventually found a small beach house in Ponte Vedra Beach that fit our budget and was only a mile from Mike's work and a half-mile walk to the Atlantic Ocean. As soon as the realtor drove up in front of the house for the first visit, the long, winding sidewalk leading to the front door immediately caught my eye. And, the house had a small, beautiful lake in the back yard, surrounded with protected Florida Guana Preserve. The house even came with its own private beach access! Though when the kids were little we didn't walk to our private beach much, because the kids preferred being at the Inn & Club, where their dad worked. Also, both kids were busy with school, and their chosen after-school activities did not include hanging out at the beach; neither Jesse nor Nicki were interested in surfing like a lot of the kids in the area were.

Instead, both kids were swimming and playing tennis—a *lot* of tennis. Mike made sure that Jesse and Nicki had tennis racquets even before they began walking. He first taught them how to catch a tennis ball in their hands by tossing balls to them; I was amazed watching their small hands catch the yellow felt tennis balls. They always tried so hard to please him and make him proud—they were so polite and respectful at every age. As soon as they could walk, he taught them how to grip a tennis racquet and eventually make contact with the ball perfectly in the center of the strings.

As they progressed, Mike would take them out on the tennis court to play running games and side-to-side drills with them. When the kids were ten years old they began competing in local tournaments, and we enrolled them in all-day summer tennis camps at the Association of Tennis

Professional headquarters in Ponte Vedra Beach. When Jesse was twelve, he and his dad began playing together in father-son tournaments, as well as national tournaments. But as the children got older, I knew that tennis was not going to be either of their athletic destinies, and in fact they both quit playing when they were about fifteen, and instead increased their involvement in the performing arts. Yet even though Jesse and Nicki chose performing arts as their career goals, I was thankful that their father had already—through athletics—instilled a strong work ethic in both of them. Mike supported Jesse as he went on to train and compete in martial arts, where he earned several international medals in Jiu Jitsu, his preferred sport; and, Mike was always proud of Nicki for her commitment to acting, dancing, and singing.

Jesse was not only athletic—he was also musically talented. When he was eight years old, he found my worn-out acoustic guitar in our hall closet and asked me if I would teach him how to play it. Since it had been a long time since I'd played my guitar, Mike and I agreed to sign Jesse up for weekly guitar lessons at his grammar school. We warned him that if he didn't practice, his lessons would stop. But, not only did he practice for *hours* after school and on the weekends, his teacher called to let us know that he had to move Jesse ahead in his lessons and advance him to book *four* by the end of the first month! Jesse was definitely a rock star back then, and to fit the image he grew his hair long and learned to play songs by Nirvana, Ozzy Osbourne, and Metallica—just to name a few.

Jesse's technique was so good that, when he was thirteen, he entered a guitar contest at a large music store in Orlando. He had studied and learned to play rock, jazz, and classical guitar, and at the competition he showcased all those skills in front of a crowd of spectators and several judges. Mike, Nicki, and I were so proud of Jesse when the judges announced him as the winner in front of a full crowd of spectators. He was elated when the judges brought him up on stage and presented him with a new candy-apple-red electric Ibanez guitar, along with several packs of guitar strings, foot pedals, and other musical prizes. I knew then that my son, with this victory, had confirmed another of his passions in life.

Nicki had her own passions early on, too. When she was four, she began pre-ballet lessons; then, as she grew older, she expanded with vocal lessons, gymnastics, and all forms of dance: lyrical, modern, jazz, ballet, and hip-hop. She knew it was important to hone diverse skills if she wanted to pursue musical theater. Everyone involved in performing arts would remind students of the necessity to become a "triple threat": that is, to be an artist strong in acting, singing, and all forms of dance. Nicki aspired to become famous one day, so at age ten she began vocal lessons. But, she always loved acting more than singing and dancing, so she jumped at every opportunity to audition for shows in our community theater.

Both children attended the public school system for middle school in Ponte Vedra Beach, but as they had a strong passion for the performing arts, they auditioned—first Jesse, followed by Nicki—to attend high school at Douglas Anderson School of the Arts (DASOTA) in downtown Jacksonville. When each respectively got the call letting them know they'd passed their entrance exams, they were ecstatic, and I was unbelievably proud that they'd earned their own way into their dream school through their work ethic and passion for the arts.

Jesse paved the way two years before Nicki, starting his freshman year by joining the Music Department and later the jazz band; Nicki started her tenure at DASOTA in the Theater Department. When Jesse began his freshman year, I immediately got involved and volunteered to chaperone many of the trips out of town for their competitions and performances; I also served on the PTA and the Theater Scholarship Committee. Both kids were always respectful to Mike and me, and I appreciated that they let us share in their goals and dreams.

Although they both had to commute fifteen miles to school, and necessarily had to leave behind their many neighborhood friends from elementary and middle school, both kids had a passion for the performing arts that needed to be recognized and developed; the choice was 100 percent their decision. And the choice wasn't difficult: there was never a question in their minds, even in middle school, about where they wanted to attend high school.

As it turned out, though, Nicki was destined to stay very close to her hometown friends even while she made new friends at DASOTA; Nicki had no problem with the transition to her new school. I was so proud of her while as she pursued her lifelong dreams of performance: every day she studied and worked hard, and auditioned for every performance that she could. In these kinds of high schools, it's quite the norm for freshmen and sophomores to have to work their way up to the actual performance level, so Nicki's freshman year was mainly spent backstage, helping with makeup and costumes; but through it all, she never complained. Nicki loved all of it, always trying to learn every aspect of theater from—and looking up to—the junior and senior acting students, all while waiting patiently for her time to shine on stage. She never once regretted the choice to pursue her dreams at a performing arts high school, and looked forward to every opportunity that DASOTA would offer her.

One day, Nicki called me from school, elated. "Mommy," she cried with joy, "I got a part in the musical *Rags!*"

I knew that she had auditioned for a part in the play several weeks before, as she'd had to stay several days after school for the auditions; and at home, I had listened happily to her when she practiced her lines. When Dr. Beger announced the cast for the show, Nicki couldn't wait until she made it home to tell me: she was so excited and happy. Even though she would have to stay after school every day for months for practice, and attend rehearsals on the weekends, she didn't care. Nicki loved that, even though she was just a sophomore, her hard work had already earned her a part in a show. It was a huge honor.

And, it got even better: a number of other Florida high schools had competed to earn a spot performing a musical at the Theatre Tallahassee; for weeks we had all been on pins and needles waiting for the big announcement. So, when Nicki burst through the front door after school one day, threw her book bag on the table, then grabbed me up and hugged me tight, yelling with happiness, "We get to perform *Rags* at State, Mommy!" I began to shed tears of joy for her. The cast of *Rags* had been selected to go to Tallahassee that April and perform the production in front of several other performing arts high schools' staff and students! Nicki's dreams were coming true. Additionally, Jesse would be going on this trip as well, as the DASOTA orchestra—in which he played guitar—would be performing the music for the production. Because I served on the Boosters Club, I was asked by the instrumental music department director to go with the students as a chaperone. I agreed—which probably didn't thrill either of my children at the time, having Mom as a chaperone!—but they never objected.

It was there, in Tampa, that many of us noticed the first definite sign that something was wrong with Nicki. The students had been practicing on the main stage theater in Tampa for several days, excitedly getting ready for their big Friday-night performance. Dr. Lee Beger, head of the theater department (nicknamed "Doc" by the students), gave the cast most of Friday off, telling the students to all meet in the theater at 4:00 pm for a dress rehearsal before the show's evening performance at 8:00. Doc had never had a problem before with students running late for rehearsal; all her students loved her, but they also knew that if they were late, they'd better have a legitimate excuse—or they might have to wait a long time to get into another show! Like the rest of the students, Nicki loved and respected Doc, so I was very concerned when she didn't show up for rehearsal. This wasn't like her at all. Not only was Nicki highly reliable, but she had also been selected as a sophomore to perform with the juniors and seniors in the show: this was a privilege, and she knew it. She lived to perform. As I sat in the auditorium waiting for her to show up for dress rehearsal, all I could think was: where *was* she?

Everyone in the auditorium began to ask each other if they had seen Nicki, but no one knew where she was. Eventually we determined that no one had seen her the entire day except for her roommate, who'd left the hotel room at 9:00 that morning while Nicki was still sleeping. When we sent her roommate back to the room to check on Nicki, she found Nicki still sound asleep. Not only that, but she had a hard time waking her. When Nicki finally woke up and realized that she was late for rehearsal, she was embarrassed and terribly upset: she couldn't understand how she'd slept until 4:30 in the afternoon. She was so confused; nothing like this had ever happened before. Growing up, Nicki had gone to a lot of sleepovers, at which she and her girlfriends had stayed up all night and coming home exhausted, but even in those situations she'd never slept until this late in the afternoon. What was going on?

Nicki knew that oversleeping was not an acceptable excuse for being late for any show or rehearsal. Once she understood the situation, she pulled herself together and went to the auditorium for rehearsal. Doc was obviously disappointed, and stopped the rehearsal to lecture Nicki on stage in front of all the cast. Nicki started to sob, which baffled me—a lecture from Doc wasn't something to laugh or smile about, but it sure wasn't anything that would normally have made Nicki cry. What was wrong? Why was Nicki so emotional? My heart ached for her as I sat in the theater, watching. I could tell that the other students felt bad for her too, but I think we all assumed that she was just unusually tired. After Doc's chewing-out, Nicki gathered herself and joined the rehearsal. She seemed okay on the surface, but underneath her poise I could tell that she was still confused and extremely upset.

Despite all the commotion the rehearsal went well, the show that evening was magnificent, and Nicki's performance was exceptional. After the show, the students partied for the rest of the night, giddy that the show—and all their hard work—had been a success. And, best of all, it seemed like Nicki had recovered completely. On Sunday we headed back to Jacksonville with a bus full of tired students. Nicki, in the seat next to me, laid her head on my lap and slept the entire way home. I thought it was a little odd that she was *so* tired, but I figured it was because of her hectic schedule. Actually, when I looked around the bus, *everyone* seemed worn out from the week of rehearsals and from staying up all night. Most of the kids slept for the entire ride.

Yet even back at home, Nicki never seemed to fully recover from that week's events. After going back to school the next day, Nicki told me that one of her good friends had noticed such a change in her personality that she'd asked if Nicki was doing drugs. Doing *drugs*? This accusation bothered her, and obviously me too. And then another friend, a boy at school, said that he'd also noticed Nicki didn't seem quite the same; he confided in her that he suffered from depression but had gotten help, and suggested that Nicki might like to talk to someone. With this in mind, we discussed the possibility with Nicki that depression was causing her problems, but we both knew somehow that wasn't it. I hoped that Nicki's situation would improve once school was out for the summer, since she would be able to rest.

At this point, Nicki was sleeping even more and seemed to become fatigued more easily, even by small activities. She'd always had a sharp memory but now she seemed to start forgetting things; additionally, she was having frequent headaches. When I told her to take Tylenol, she admitted that she'd been taking a lot of Tylenol already but it wasn't working. Obviously, I was unbelievably concerned, and told Mike right away—but our communication had fractured so much that I don't think he listened or really believed what I was saying. As a stay-at-home mom, I'd spent a lot of time over the years volunteering my services at the school, and had put all my efforts into raising our children and helping with their activities rather than, frankly, spending time with my husband. When Nicki suddenly began having these unexplainable headaches and bizarre confusion problems, her father was concerned, of course, but as he wasn't normally involved in her day-to-day life like I was, he couldn't really see things up close.

Maybe the vagueness of her symptoms was why I threw every bit of my energy into figuring out what was wrong; I spent all my time with Nicki, except for when she was at school or social events like sleepovers. During this period, Mike was working most of the time, and with the way I was focusing on Nicki, my husband and I really started to drift apart from each other. Perhaps he was jealous that he wasn't getting any attention from me. I tried to keep him informed with what was going on, but everything—Nicki's confusion symptoms; my need to take care of her; the stressful atmosphere in our home—just brought more tension and strife to our marriage. I know I was neglecting my husband—and my son Jesse as well—but he wasn't being supportive at all to either Nicki or me. I felt completely alone.

Since we didn't have any clue what could be causing the problems—exhaustion, forgetfulness—Mike thought it would help if Nicki stayed as busy as possible. I wasn't sure about it, as I thought Nicki should rest more, but he was insistent that she should get a job. Nicki knew that things weren't going so well between her dad and me, so—since she wanted to please her dad, and make it easier for me—she began looking for a job right away. This bothered me, because I was worried about her mental confusion and how tired she always was, and now there was one more thing on her plate: worrying about her parents. I felt that if she got a job it would cause her more fatigue, which in turn might make her confusion problems even worse. I knew that she needed more rest, not more activity, but we just didn't know what to do—and no matter how strange it was, I never, ever thought it could be something life threatening. I didn't want to go against my husband, but I was incredibly upset with him as well: no matter how much I tried to convince him that something was seriously wrong with our daughter, he didn't seem to be as concerned as I was. I think he thought I was just being overprotective. But I don't think that was the case: if he had been with Nicki the amount of time I was, he would have seen there was something very wrong with her.

Yet even if I thought my husband was wrong, it wasn't easy too stand up to him on anything. So, I went against my instincts and drove Nicki around town, waiting in the car while she filled out job applications, hoping that no one would hire her. Nicki had an engaging personality, and she was so smart, so I was disappointed but not very surprised when she was offered a job at Publix Supermarket as a cashier almost immediately; she accepted the job even before school was out. After completing her training, she was handed a uniform and a work schedule, and began working four days a week after school.

I worried about her while she was at work, but things

seemed fine—for two weeks. One night, Nicki came home upset and confused because the store manager had told her she needed to redo all her training, and had demoted her: she was now going to be stacking shelves instead of working the register. Poor Nicki was devastated, and felt like a failure. It was odd—she was so smart! How on earth could she work perfectly for two weeks as a cashier, only to now be demoted? I tried to come up with an explanation for these strange occurrences, but couldn't deny that my fear was growing even stronger.

All that summer, Nicki's symptoms persisted. In August, as Nicki was preparing to start her junior year of high school, Mike and I planned to drive Jesse to Miami for college: he had earned a scholarship for jazz guitar at the University of Miami. I didn't want to leave Nicki alone, but felt bad that Jesse had been neglected for months because of his sister's strange un-diagnosable illness. I begged Nicki to go with us, but she wanted to stay home to work—and frankly she just didn't feel well enough to travel. But I didn't feel right about leaving her alone, and had a sixth sense that something was terribly wrong. I loved both my children equally, but Nicki needed me. I was her mother.

But I knew that I had been neglecting my husband and my son all summer, especially since this was supposed to be Jesse's time. After all, he was moving out of the house and starting college and life on his own. I was a wreck about leaving Nicki, and I'm sure it bothered Mike too, but my son was going away to college and I wanted to see him off.

Before leaving, the four of us hugged as a family; Nicki laughed and told Jesse how much she would enjoy having the bathroom they'd shared for ten years all to herself now. Jesse had taken all of his messy stuff out of it, and Nicki noted she wasn't going to miss fighting over the shower before school. Now the mornings would be less hectic, and the bathroom would always be clean. But it was hard watching this parting. Jesse had never complained about being ignored all summer, and I could tell that he was also concerned about leaving his little sister. He was her brother, after all: he knew something was wrong. Growing up, Nicki had always followed her brother's lead. When Jesse had wanted to take karate lessons, Nicki asked to take them, too; then it was swimming, gymnastics, tennis, and soccer. Through it all, Nicki was right beside him. She looked up to her big brother, and he always treated her with love and respect.

So after all of the teasing and bantering, they hugged each other tightly, and we all knew that the parting was bittersweet.

While we were dropping Jesse off in Miami, I was worried about Nicki the whole time, and spoke constantly to her on the phone. This may have been another problem for our marriage: I could never get my mind off of Nicki, and it may have seemed like I didn't want to engage with my husband, or work on our togetherness. I loved him, but I found that I just couldn't give anything of myself to anyone besides Nicki—and by now this had been going on for a year.

When we returned from Miami, I immediately noticed a new disturbing development: Nicki was pale and had obviously lost weight; I was extremely concerned when, as

I walked through the door, the first thing she said to me was "Mommy, something is wrong with me." Nicki had never before actually expressed fear about her condition. She told me that while we were away, she'd gotten a headache so severe that her friends offered to take her to the ER, but she'd wanted to wait for me to get home. I felt terrible that she'd suffered on her own like this. So once again we went to see our primary care doctor; I had already taken her there several times—at one of our visits she fainted in the waiting room, fell out of her chair onto the floor and cut her forehead, and had a mild seizure. But all we got from that visit was a half-hour wait and a diagnosis of a "virus" from a doctor who, at our latest visit, still could not identify what was wrong. The next day Nicki felt a little better so, puzzling as it was, we thought maybe the doctor had been right and it *was* a virus. Obviously, we desperately wanted to believe we had an answer.

That August, Nicki started her junior year at DASOTA. But things still weren't right, and I wondered how she was going to manage working and going to school with everything that was going on—how could she balance it all? The next eight weeks became increasingly rough. She had to leave the house at seven in the morning for school and wouldn't get off work until ten at night, making it nearly eleven o'clock before she got home, ate dinner, started homework, and finally collapsed into bed. No wonder she was exhausted by the end of every day. I knew her schedule was too busy for a young girl, and could see that she was constantly tired and run down. I begged her to stop working but she didn't want to upset her dad, and even though I tried to talk to my husband, he wouldn't budge. It was as if Mike and I were living two separate lives; I was beginning to feel like a failure as a mother and a wife. I had no time for my husband because I was exhausted from worry, and it seemed that no one could help us. I wanted Mike to love and support me, but I began to fear that maybe he didn't love me anymore. I couldn't explain what was happening to my daughter. All I could do was pray to God for help.

One day after school, Nicki was noticeably upset and confused again. She came into the family room, dropped her book bag, and sat down on the couch beside me; she looked tired and baffled as she started telling me about what happened at school. "Mommy, what is going on with me?" she asked. I moved closer to her and put my hand on her leg. She told me that today in school, when she was called upon to recite a monologue for her final exam in front of her classmates and teachers, she had completely drawn a blank; no matter what she did, she could not remember a single word of what she had spent weeks memorizing for her exam. This was shocking, and I was terrified when she told me this. And I felt so bad when I thought of how embarrassing this must have been for her, to fumble in front of all her classmates and teachers. I knew something was horribly wrong: Nicki had always had a fantastic memory and, with all her work in drama and performance, was especially skilled at memorizing and reciting. *What was going on?*

Then, one morning before school, Nicki came into the kitchen and told me she had a headache. It was odd; she'd already mentioned having a headache before, and now she was repeating it again.

"A headache? Well just take a Tylenol," I said, trying not to sound too concerned.

She frowned. "I have been, Mommy, but they aren't working. I still have a headache when I take them. It won't go away."

Now I was scared, because this seemed more concrete than her summer of mystery symptoms. Previously, she'd told me that her eyes sometimes went blurry, but she'd had an eye exam just six months before that said she had 20/20 vision—she *couldn't* be having eye problems. When she started occasionally vomiting for no reason, we knew that something was seriously wrong, but her symptoms never happened at the same time. Because the vomiting occurred around the time of her period, we thought it might be hormonal, so I took her to an OB/GYN who thought that putting her on birth control pills might help relieve her headaches; but the pills caused her headache to spike even more, so the doctor told Nicki to stop taking them. We were so worried: just like the Tylenol for her headaches, nothing was working. A virus or mono could cause the kinds of symptoms Nicki had—someone even suggested that it could be West Nile—but her doctor couldn't determine the cause no matter how many tests they ran. Eventually, at one of her many doctor appointments, we thought we had found the cause: migraines. Migraines can make you vomit and cause confusion, so we thought it could very well be the cause. But the medication for migraines didn't relieve any of her symptoms.

Even as diagnosis after diagnosis failed us, I still never thought it could be cancer. When we realized that the doctors were confused, it scared us even more because we didn't know where else to go for help. We just carried on in our confusion, searching for answers. Strangely, we later realized that Nicki's beloved dog Lucy—named after her favorite actress, Lucille Ball—seemed to have more insight into the situation than we did. One day, as Nicki sat on the couch with her schoolbooks on her lap, Lucy jumped up on the back of the couch and began sniffing the top of Nicki's head on the left side. While we didn't take any note of it the first time, it soon became a pattern: every time Nicki sat down, Lucy would sniff around the left side of her head. Nicki loved Lucy, but it annoyed her, and she'd ask me to make the dog stop. "Why does she always do this to me?" she'd ask. I didn't know, but I suggested maybe it was the smell of her shampoo. It never occurred to me that Lucy could smell the tumor in Nicki's brain. I should have known—a beagle can smell anything!

October 3, 2002, was Nicki's seventeenth birthday, and her friends were planning a surprise for her at school. But when she got up that morning she said that she wasn't feeling well. This was a bad sign—she had been looking forward to this day for weeks. I encouraged her to go to school anyway, though, thinking maybe she would feel better once she got there. I hated to see her stay home on her birthday, especially since she'd seemed so down lately. Eventually, with my prodding, she went to go to school, even though I could tell something was wrong. But I knew she would miss out on so much if she didn't go, so she got up, got dressed, twisted her hair up in a bun, and off she went. I thought about her all day. When she walked through the door after school, carrying a handful of gifts and balloons, she seemed happier. I was glad that she didn't miss sharing her birthday with her friends, yet still I felt uneasy because I knew that something just wasn't right with her.

That night, Nicki had plans to go out for dinner with

her friend Katie, who wanted to celebrate and give Nicki a special gift—and also to speak to her privately. Katie had sensed a change in her friend and wanted to find out if there was something wrong between them. Having been her best friend for five years, Katie had obviously noticed a huge change in Nicki's personality, a change so large that she thought perhaps she'd done something wrong or that maybe, painfully, Nicki had simply outgrown their friendship.

Nicki told me all about it when she got home that evening. Over dinner, Katie had expressed her concerns. "I feel like we have been drifting apart lately," she said, "and that makes me sad. Something's different about you. If you don't want to be friends anymore, that's okay. I understand, but I wanted you to know that I'll always love you." Katie gave her a diary, suggesting that she could write about things and maybe figure out what was going on in her life.

Nicki was bothered and unnerved by their conversation, particularly by Katie's suggestion that her personality was different. She showed me the card and the journal that Katie had given to her. She was looking to me for answers, but I just didn't have any: I was as confused as she was. As her mother I wanted to take all this craziness from her, but I just didn't know how. And that powerlessness broke my heart.

Katie wasn't the only one to notice a change. Nicki's voice teacher, Priscilla, had also noticed something was wrong. Pricilla had two sons and always loved having Nicki around; she had become like a daughter to her. I would drop Nicki off at Priscilla's house once or twice a week for her lesson, and sometimes, if Nicki had had a long day or something was bothering her, she would talk to Priscilla about it. Over the six-year span of their relationship they became close, and I was glad that Nicki was close to a woman with a beautiful character, a gifted role model with whom she could talk.

At the beginning of the school year, Priscilla put together a singing group with Nicki and four of her other female pupils. They—perhaps prophetically—called themselves B.L.U.S.H., an acronym for Believing Lets Us See Heaven. The girls had long been performing in church and at other public events by this time, and enjoyed a degree of local success, even sometimes singing the national anthem for the professional baseball team in Jacksonville. The girls were even planning to perform and tour throughout Europe. But now suddenly Nicki had lost her spark, and she didn't know why.

When she came to me and told me that she didn't want to be in the group anymore I was surprised: this was her passion. Plus, her best friend Katie was in the group, and the girls all knew that without Nicki BLUSH would disband. Nicki didn't want to break up the group, but she said that she just didn't want to do it anymore. She was always so tired and didn't want to go to practice. Priscilla, obviously concerned, talked to Nicki and me about her disinterest and the changes in her personality; none of us could figure out why Nicki's sparky, fun, and peppy spirit had vanished. She was totally changed, but no one—even Nicki herself— understood what was going on with her. With great sympathy for Nicki's struggle, Priscilla felt that the change in Nicki was so dramatic that we should all support her decision to leave the group, and that we should not expect her to continue. The other four girls were disappointed that their days of performing together were over, of course, but they understood that something was wrong with Nicki and supported her as a friend despite her sudden departure from the group. Everyone went on with their lives, and Nicki's hidden disease remained a mystery.

Then one day Nicki called me from school sounding desperate. I knew that she needed help right away, and immediately jumped in the car, picked her up from school, and took her again to see our primary doctor. When we arrived, Nicki and I took the only two empty chairs in the waiting area. I was so nervous because I wasn't sure that Nicki was going to be able to wait very long—it seemed like she could hardly sit up in her chair. Then, as she went to lean her head on my shoulder, she fell right out of her chair onto the floor, hitting her head hard enough to break the skin on her forehead. With her forehead cut and bleeding, lying on the floor, she began to go into a seizure. A nurse rushed out to put her in a wheelchair, then took us into a room in the back where we had to wait another twenty minutes for the doctor to see her. I was terrified. When the doctor finally came in to examine her, he still couldn't determine what was wrong, so he sent us home with instructions that if she continued to vomit or felt ill the next morning, then we should take her to the emergency room at our local hospital.

Of course, she wasn't better the next morning, so we took her to the ER. Inside the waiting room, it was chaos: babies crying; a middle-aged man bleeding; a teenage girl with what appeared to be a broken arm; and Nicki, who was so weak that she couldn't sit up alone. Mike held her on his lap and cradled her head while we waited anxiously for her to be seen. I remember they asked Nicki a series of questions about her pain level, asking her to rate it on a scale of one to ten. She told them her pain felt like a "five." I protested, arguing that Nicki was actually at a level ten, but the attendant took Nicki's word and not mine, so we ended up waiting for over an hour. I didn't think Nicki would make it through the wait. When she was finally brought back to be seen by a doctor, we explained what had been going on with her the past weeks. The immediate problem was that she was dehydrated from not eating and from all the vomiting. Mike and I sat beside her bed and watched as the doctor put in IVs to administer fluids for dehydration and anti-nausea medication.

We were in the emergency room for two hours, and at the end of that time the ER doctor didn't have a clue about what was wrong with her. So, once again, they sent us home. They told us that it was probably a virus, and we should just let it run its course. Even as Nicki continued to vomit while in her wheelchair waiting to leave the hospital, they said there was nothing else they could do. It was just a virus, they insisted. But I knew that wasn't right because she had been given anti-nausea medicine and it should have stopped her from vomiting. No one seemed to take our concern and desperation seriously.

At home I made a bed for her beside me so I could monitor her throughout the night. I woke several times and, in the dark, looked at my daughter lying beside me, so frail, not moving at all. I knew she was trying to stay still because of the headache. She wasn't sleeping at all. She continued to get progressively weaker and more lethargic as dawn approached. I went over everything in my mind, desperate and terrified. Why would no one take this seriously? Why were we sent home from the hospital? We were at a loss; we had no idea what to do.

Two days after our trip to the emergency room, my life changed forever. On October 6, 2002, I woke up to find Nicki incoherent, so sick that she couldn't lift her head or open her eyes. At this point, we had exhausted all of our resources but one: Mike carried her out to the car, and we drove to Wolfson Children's Hospital in downtown Jacksonville. Why hadn't I thought of the Children's Hospital? We had never been told to take her there before. I don't know why it didn't occur to me—before now, my kids were never sick. I just hadn't known what to do. When we arrived at Wolfson, Mike once again took her in his arms and carried her into the emergency room; I walked beside them, feeling like I was going to be sick. When we entered the emergency room, Nicki looked like a rag doll, dangling from her father's strong arms, her head bobbing and her long blond hair matted and stringy. As we approached the counter, the triage nurse took one look at Nicki dangling, lifeless in her father's strong arms, and knew our daughter needed immediate attention. She hurried to us with a wheelchair, the expression on her face concerned. As soon as Mike put Nicki in the wheelchair she slumped right over; I had to hold her head up while we headed into the examining room, as well as when the nurse got her vital signs. Mike and I struggled to help her stand to get her weight.

After the nurse took her blood pressure and temperature, she was given a room, and, once there, the ER doctor immediately ordered a CT scan of her brain. I wondered why no one had suggested this before. While we waited in agony for the results, Mike and I never spoke, waiting silently. It bothered me that I now had to worry about him in addition to worrying about Nicki. It seemed as though my whole world was collapsing before me. All I wanted was that, finally, here and now, we would find out what had caused our daughter's confusion, pain, and suffering over these past six months.

Never leaving her side, we lovingly caressed Nicki's arm as she lay quietly in the cold, dimly lit hospital room. She had not moved a muscle and remained silent, in excruciating pain: her doctor couldn't give her any medicine until he found out the results. She was in so much pain—we all were. I held her hand as what seemed like a whole lifetime passed by, waiting for the results. We were anxious, eager to get the results, yet apprehensive about what they might be. I silently prayed, over and over, the entire time: please, God. Please give us some answers and please take away her pain. You can make everything all right.

When the doctor came in and asked Mike and I to step out of Nicki's room and into the hall, my first thought was I couldn't leave Nicki alone. Then fear set in, and I wondered why he wasn't giving us the results in her room—why couldn't Nicki hear too? I needed to brace myself for what was coming: I knew now at least one of my prayers would be answered. I numbly walked through the doorway, leaving my little girl alone for the first time in months. I couldn't think; I was already going into shock. So when the doctor told us that the CT scan had revealed a large tumor in Nicki's brain, I was so worn and weak that I dropped to the floor. But I had to go to her; I had to compose myself. I had made it this far, and now I knew what I feared the most was true: the answer to our question was something horrible. I got up, went into the hospital room, and took Nicki's hand. I stayed by her bedside, praying unceasingly for God's mercy. I didn't feel like myself anymore. How could this have happened right before my very eyes? Nicki was so sick, and in so much pain that she couldn't ask any questions at that time.

The doctor arranged to have Nicki immediately taken by ambulance to Shands Hospital at the University of Florida in Gainesville, two hours away, where a pediatric neurosurgeon was waiting to examine her. I rode in the ambulance with Nicki and a nurse, who was there to monitor her the whole way. I sat alone, huddled in a corner in the back, staring at my baby lying on the stretcher. I was still in shock. All I did was pray: Dear God, what are we getting into? How can this be? How can she have a brain tumor? Why didn't our primary care doctor send us here? Why didn't the emergency room doctor do a CAT scan—how could a doctor send her home vomiting, dehydrated, and with a brain tumor? Why did I let the doctor send us home? I'm terrified, this must be a nightmare; I want to wake up and find my child well. God, if I'm not just dreaming, please heal her so she can come home. This is my *baby*. You have to heal her. You *have* to fix this. I knew something was wrong, but a brain tumor? I feel like such a horrible mother for not knowing what to do. Oh, God, this can't be. Please comfort her and don't let her be afraid and please, God, *please* heal her.

Mike followed the ambulance in our car after calling Jesse to give him the heartbreaking news. Jesse's girlfriend, Kathy, and her mother drove all the way to Miami to pick

Jesse up and bring him to Gainesville to be with his family. When we arrived at Shands, I looked at Nicki lying on the stretcher; she now looked so much younger to me, so fragile and innocent. She was my baby. I watched over her closely while the paramedics wheeled her into a very large room in the ICU.

When Jesse arrived, for the first time since her crisis started Nicki seemed relieved that we were all together. We gave her the news about the tumor—though we still didn't know that the tumor was malignant; at least she knew that she would now be taken care of. Once we were all situated, her doctor came in to talk with her: he was young and handsome, in his thirties, with a warm and caring bedside manner. As he sat beside Nicki's bed, we all gathered around to listen. The doctor spoke softly but seriously to her, gently explaining that she had a large tumor in her brain, and this was what had been causing her confusion, headaches, and vomiting for the past six months. He went on to explain that he would not be able to remove the tumor because the tumor had woven itself throughout her brain tissue, making it too dangerous to cut out, though he assured her that he would be able to make her feel better by inserting a cerebral shunt: a valve that would run from her brain into her stomach to drain the excess fluid and release the pressure that was causing her headaches and vomiting. When he reached out to touch her arm, as a gesture of reassurance, we all knew that he was sincere. Next he told her that he would perform a biopsy to identify the tumor, also explaining that there were different kinds and grades of tumors, and that by tomorrow he would know for sure which she had. While sitting beside Nicki as she lay in the stark hospital bed, the doctor spoke frankly but with compassion, and I was thankful that God had provided a surgeon with such a gentle spirit, someone who could finally give us some answers. Nicki, for her part, was relieved to know that the strange weakness and forgetfulness of the past six months hadn't been her fault. Even though she hadn't said she was afraid, she had been sick and worried for so long that now all she could feel was relief. She was still exhausted, but seemed more relaxed. Finally, she was going to be taken care of. Our whole family was together with her. And even though her condition was life-threatening, she was thankful to finally know what was wrong with her.

Since there were no beds for family or visitors in the ICU, the three of us slept on the tile floor in her room. But we didn't care about our discomfort: we just wanted to be with Nicki, to assure her that she would never be alone. The next morning, as Nicki was wheeled away for surgery, my heart sank with worry. But Nicki was her theatrical self and, turning to us with a smile, flashed a thumbs-up sign. I prayed with all my heart that not only would she survive the operation, but that the tumor would be curable.

At least part of my prayer was answered when Nicki came through her surgery okay. We had to wait several hours to see her while she recovered, and when the nurse finally informed us that we could see her, we all ran to her room as fast as we could! It was difficult to see the physical after-effects of the surgery; Nicki's pretty little face was twice its normal size, and her head was swollen, especially her eyes. The pain medication made her hyper and upbeat, which would take hours to wear off, but she was so happy to see us. Her nurse had raised the back of her bed up so that she was in a sitting position, and the first thing that she said when we entered her room was, "Don't worry, guys, I feel worse than I look." But we all knew what she meant.

It took until the next morning for the results of the tumor to be conclusive; we waited anxiously for the biopsy results, pacing the floor and dying inside from impatience. When Nicki's doctor arrived, we gathered around, scared and uneasy but ready for answers. Nicki never took her eyes off the doctor while he gently explained that the tumor was malignant: a stage-four glioblastoma multiforme. I saw the sadness and concern on her face. She then looked directly at the doctor and asked, "How long do I have?"

The doctor paused and dropped his head, hesitating to answer such a blunt question from this young, beautiful girl. But then he lifted his head and, in a low tone, he answered. "One to three years. But, then, I'm not God, Nicki—so who am I to say?"

He assured her that he was going to do everything in his power to save her life, and that he would talk to us about treatment options. Reaching out, he touched Nicki's hand; I felt like he wanted to let her know that he understood the seriousness of her situation, and to acknowledge that he knew she was a mature and bright young lady. We all knew that he was sincere in his care and concern. He then asked Nicki if she had any other questions, and she shook her head no. And with that, the doctor left, while we remained in stunned silence.

This was the beginning of the end.

It was cancer in control now.

SEARCHING FOR ANSWERS

After her surgery, Mike, Jesse, and I were ready to take Nicki home and start helping her recover. I would monitor her from home, with a set schedule to administer her medications—and there were a lot. She would have to take steroids, seizure medication, and oral chemotherapy, and I needed to take her back to the hospital for blood work once a week. Reality was sinking in: my daughter had cancer. I thought about when my dad was diagnosed with colon cancer; he had been forty-nine, I was twenty-seven. I moved home to help my mom take care of him during that time, as he needed care twenty-four hours a day, and, with all that was required for his care, it was too hard for my mom to do it on her own. I helped her, even learning how to administer morphine to help with my father's pain during his final weeks. So I had some experience with cancer care, but this was different. Nicki was my baby.

My head was reeling, and I was consumed with fear, but I knew that I had to pull myself together and accept the truth. Yet at the same time, how could I? Accepting the truth would mean that this was really happening, and instead I wanted to wake up and discover this was just a horrible dream. Even with an answer, I was more confused than ever. We'd already seen Nicki change from a vivacious, healthy teenager to a very sick girl, right in front of our eyes. And now the reality of what we were facing was devastating. Everything in our lives had changed. Adjusting to our new circumstances would be hard to do, but I tried to be thankful that she was at least coming home. I prayed that she would recover completely, while knowing that we had a long road ahead of us.

It was difficult for another reason, too. At a time when I most needed Mike's support, we were completely divided. I wanted him to hold me; I wanted for all of us to embrace Nicki as a family, to reassure her that we will all be together throughout this—but it didn't happen that way. For some reason, Mike and I just couldn't sit down and talk together: we never even hugged each other, or confided in one another. I was losing him and knew it, but I couldn't help it. Taking care of Nicki was all that I had energy for, and I didn't get the sense that he was going to support me in any way. I knew that Mike needed me too, but I couldn't give him anything. Every day he got up and went to work, and I was left alone to deal with our daughter's day-to-day doctor's visits, hospitals stays, and all the medications that I had to give to her without knowing how they might affect her. I felt responsible for her entire life: I was her full-time caretaker, and I was *scared*. I tried to remember that Jesse still needed a mother too, and tried to find time to spend with him, but even my son had to come second, though he was never second in my heart. Jesse was so understanding, and tried to help in any way he could, easing my tension by allowing me to concentrate on her. My love for my children was equal under any and all circumstances, including these. But I was going to be there for her no matter what during this time, because Nicki needed her mommy, and I needed her too.

But it was different with my marriage. Mike and I were drifting apart at this critical time; it felt like my life was spinning out of control, and I couldn't even remember the last time I felt close to my husband. We were both hurting, but we certainly were not a team. My desire, time, and intimacy as a wife just weren't there, and Mike wasn't helping to bring the desire for intimacy back. All my energy had to go to Nicki, and if there was any left over, Jesse got it. I thought that once Nicki got better, Jesse and I could make up for lost time. But with Mike, it felt as though time had already run out. So, as everything crumbled around me, I put all of my energy into loving my daughter and taking care of her needs, just trying not to worry about anything else—even if it was my marriage.

Before leaving the hospital to return back home to Jacksonville, Nicki and I had been introduced to the radiologist/oncologist who would be administering radiation treatments. Once again, the doctor was sensitive and gentle, a woman who had daughters of her own about Nicki's age; she told Nicki that she could call her Dr. Nancy. Nicki seemed comfortable with her right away, and I felt that she was another gift from God. Dr. Nancy explained to Nicki that she would need six weeks of daily radiation treatment, and after that her chemotherapy would continue every three weeks. Because of her brain surgery, Nicki would also need to take medications at home, such as Zofran—an anti-seizure medication—for nausea, and steroids to keep her brain from swelling. Her doctors also informed us that we would need to find a pediatric oncologist as well as a neurologist back home in Jacksonville.

It was all mind-boggling to me. I still couldn't quite believe that the strange symptoms she had been experiencing were caused by a brain tumor. And I was still trying to wrap my brain around the fact that she could die. I began to be obsessed with finding out what had caused the brain tumor. Had I done something wrong? Were Mike and I responsible for something that could have contributed to this terrible disease? I wondered what he was thinking about everything, but when I tried to talk to him he just wouldn't communicate at all, instead leaving the room. As Mike and I continued to become more distant with each passing day, I poured more and more of my efforts into Nicki, helping her to get back to a more normal teenage life. But that was almost impossible, since her life now was comprised of trips to the clinic and hospital, treatments, and blood draws. She wasn't able to see many of her friends during this time, either, because they were in school, and afterward, when they had time, she was exhausted from her treatments. We both hoped that eventually she would be able to get some of her normal life back, but that seemed such a long way off.

Our lives continued to change dramatically. Jesse returned to college in Miami, but he worried constantly about Nicki, and tried to help her every way he could by traveling back and forth to see her as much as he could. And even though he never spoke to me about it, I'm sure he was also concerned about Mike and I. I missed him so much, but I believed that we all needed to resume our lives as normally as possible, especially Jesse. I couldn't believe that Jesse had graduated high school and started college. This was supposed to be the best time of his young life—but of course it wasn't. Both of our children were being deprived of any normalcy during this time; how long ago was it that we were all on a schedule that made sense? I tried to keep up with Jesse's life while he was in Miami, but it was hard, especially when I knew that even though he wasn't living at home, he still needed me. I tried to find time for him, but it just wasn't there. All I could do was pray that God would watch over my son and keep him safe.

A week after Nicki's first surgery, we started making the daily trip back and forth to Gainesville for her radiation treatments. One day while driving, I thought about the day she was born: October 3, 1985. We named her Nicolette Beverly Leach—Beverly after my mother. My baby girl was perfect! The first time I held her, she wrapped her tiny hand around my finger as if to say, "Hold on to me, Mommy!"—and I felt like I had for all these years: blessed by God to have been given two healthy children. Jesse was turning two when Nicki was born, and in my eyes God had given us the perfect family. First a healthy boy, and now a beautiful healthy girl—what more could I want in life? As they grew from babies to children, they were so caring and kind, and they gave me such incredible joy.

But as my mind returned to the present, I began to think about the future and what it might hold for our family. Nicki and I never talked much during these rides in the car to radiation. We just listened to music—it was a boring two-hour ride each way. But I always wondered, when we weren't talking, what was going through her head. Keeping my mind in the present was a challenge; I couldn't believe that our lives had changed to this. I just wanted her to get past this so she could get better, get back to school, and be a normal teenager again. But, underneath the hope, I knew that soon the radiation would make her tired all the time, and her hair would fall out. It seemed so long ago that she was healthy. When my once-vibrant and once-healthy daughter began to vomit from her cancer treatment, and we were warned she could have seizures despite her medication, I knew it was going to be hard to make the transition to our new life.

I was struggling with the reality of our situation. I didn't want to be sad around her, but how could I pretend otherwise? I *wasn't* happy. I didn't want to show it or have her see it, but I was dying inside. Nicki had enough to deal with—she didn't need to worry about her mother, even though I knew she did. I had to be strong for her. I thought that if I could just *act* normal, everything would be *like* normal—but it didn't work because nothing *was* normal anymore. And I wasn't sure that I would ever recognize normal again after experiencing this. I wanted to move out of the present moment because it was so terrifying, and yet the future was even more uncertain.

The first day we returned to the hospital for treatments, I was eager to ask Nicki's doctors what could have possibly caused the tumor. I needed to know if something like being dropped on her head could have made something go wrong in her brain. They assured me that bumps to her head or multiple doses of antibiotics hadn't caused her tumor. Maybe they just didn't know. But I still wonder today if research can identify a head injury early in a child's life as a precursor to developing a brain tumor later in life.

Though they were firm, the doctors had only temporarily reassured me that I hadn't done something to cause my daughter's cancer: I obsessed about it the whole ride home, while Nicki sat beside me listening to music. Could it have been caused by smelling paint vapors? We had painted her crib when she was a baby, and she slept in it for a full year. Could it be the paint from the crib? Or, her bedroom—we had painted it twice when she was in grade school. Could that be it? Or what about that visit to her grandparents in Boston when she was six, and we all swam in Walden Pond? She contracted impetigo from the water and was in bed for two weeks with a high fever. Her skin was red and blotchy, and her recovery seemed to take forever. Wait—maybe it was that birthday party in middle school when that mother let the girls suck in helium from the balloons so their voices would get high. I was like a dog with a bone, revisiting every tiny occurrence that I could think of.

Nicki and I tried to keep busy doing fun things when we weren't traveling to her treatments, but since we were so tired most of the time we would just relax at home, watching movies and talking. In fact, we talked a lot. Nicki had a lot of questions, of course, and I knew that she was searching for answers just as I was.

It made me sad when, one evening while we were sitting together on the couch as we always did, Nicki told me that she thought her brain tumor was probably caused at conception. She began to ask me questions about my dad's cancer. It seemed sad that this was what prompted her to ask about him. She knew that he had died from cancer at forty-nine, but that was about all I had told my children about their grandfather. I remember that she turned to look at me, and with a serious tone said, "I think I've had this gene since I was a baby. Something must have gone wrong when I was conceived."

This caught me by such surprise that I didn't ask her to elaborate. I felt guilty that maybe it was *me* who was responsible for her cancer, especially since my dad had cancer and died so young. Was that what she was thinking? This was a silent fear of mine: maybe some cancer gene had skipped his children but had found its way to one of his grandchildren. It broke my heart! So I asked her oncologist at the children's clinic if she could have been born with this tumor, or if it was possibly in her brain from a young age and just started growing when she was a teen. When I asked, he immediately told me that this kind of tumor was fast growing and had developed very recently—she could not have had this tumor from birth. But I still wondered.

One day, Nicki and I were watching an episode of Dr. Phil. It was about a fifteen-year-old mother who had gotten pregnant in high school. As I was watching the show I was thinking, *you don't have a crisis*. Getting pregnant while you're a teenager is not a crisis. We could have handled that easily—try having to battle a deadly tumor in your brain as a teenager. Try fighting for your life—*this* is a crisis. The teenage mother on the show had been unable to bring her baby with her because it was too young at the time, and her doctors had warned her not to. While the show didn't explain what the reason was, I assumed it was because a newborn can contract viruses and colds while traveling. When Nicki heard that, she turned to me and asked, "Mommy, how old was I when you took me to Sweden?"

I was thinking the exact same thing when she said that. In fact, I was remembering that trip and how hard it was with a two-year-old and a two-week-old baby, both in diapers. The four of us always stayed in one hotel room to save money, and I had to keep the kids busy while Mike slept because we were on different time zones. It was tricky: Mike needed to rest before his matches, so I had to watch the babies all night long because they were wide awake. I remembered that the drinking water was different than what Nicki was used to at home, and it gave her a tummy ache; she had been pretty irritable on that trip.

After thinking for a moment, I answered. "You were

three weeks old. But your doctors said that it was okay to take you on the plane, so we did."

Was that a sign? Why had this happened? I had never heard of not flying with a baby before. Could that early trip with my baby, when she was only a few weeks old, have possibly caused her to develop a brain tumor?

Her question, though, made me realize that Nicki was also searching for answers. We weren't alone in our search—it was kind of like getting justice when you or a loved one has been assaulted. I wanted closure, and I needed to know if there was anything I had missed or could have done differently to prevent this from happening to Nicki or to anyone else. I was supposed to protect her; I was her *mother*. But apparently, I couldn't protect her from cancer. Indeed, nobody can, at least until doctors discover prevention or a cure.

As I had already witnessed my dad's death from colon cancer in 1980, I thought that I knew how hard the road would be as I walked down it again with my daughter. But I soon realized that even my dad's cancer wasn't going to devastate me as much as Nicki's. I had eventually learned to accept my dad's death, but I knew that if my daughter died, I would never heal from it.

CANCER IS NOW IN CONTROL

When Nicki's doctor told her that she possibly had only one to three years left to live, she made the decision to accept the journey, however long it would be, with dignity, strength, and determination. Like many other teenagers and young adults who get cancer, she was filled with hope and remained incredibly positive, even telling me, while leaving the hospital after receiving her first round of radiation, that she wasn't going to die from this tumor. It was her optimism that helped me put my search for answers to rest. It was cancer; we had done nothing to cause it; and now it was time to accept that and do our best to beat it. I looked to Nicki as an example of positive thinking, but I didn't find it easy. I kept my hope for a miracle alive by praying unceasingly and trusting God.

Because of Nicki's outgoing personality, she had many great friends. They missed her, and would take time to call her while they were at school. I was anxious, though. Sure, they were concerned, and they were worried about her, but I also knew that the constant calls would slow down as soon as they got used to not having Nicki around anymore. I wanted her to be around her friends and not isolated, sitting at home with me; I worried that, once they stopped calling, she could become depressed. But she was just too sick to go back to school and, soon enough, as time went by, she missed her whole junior year. What were we going to do every day? This was the hardest part, and one of my most sorrowful fears for her: being isolated from her peers and stuck at home with Mom.

One afternoon, I was sitting at the kitchen counter,

watching Nicki make a sandwich. We had just returned home from radiation in Gainesville, and Nicki was hungry. Our original goal during the six weeks back and forth was to hit every fast food restaurant along the way, but we had quickly gotten over that bad idea and instead always came home to eat. In the background on the radio we could hear the song "The Voice Within," by Christina Aguilera. We were silent as Christina belted out the emotional lyrics: "You will learn to begin / to trust the voice within."

When she heard that, Nicki turned to me, suddenly sobbing, and said, "Mommy, I'm ruined." I jumped down from my stool and held her as we both broke down and cried. These breakdowns were rare for Nicki, but when they happened they were heartbreaking, though she always seemed to recover soon and would get back on track. Although I didn't ask her what she meant when she said "I'm ruined," I knew her well enough—she loved acting and performing, and now she was having memory problems because of the tumor's location. "Chemo brain" is real: cancer treatments, especially for brain tumors, can cause memory, speech, vision, and balance problems, depending on where the tumor is located. Even though radiation oncologists do everything they can to radiate only the diseased brain tissue, it still is very hard to avoid hitting normal healthy brain. Nicki was smart enough to know that her treatments were creating even more vision and memory problems.

During this time I continued to feel alone and isolated from the world as I knew it. My marriage just wasn't improving over time as I had hoped; Mike would leave for work and I'd spent every waking hour with Nicki. There didn't seem to be a world outside of hospitals and clinics.

Nicki and I saw many other cancer patients who were also fighting for their lives, and I understood that this constant struggle seemed to be the norm in our new world of doctor visits, treatments, and procedures. I was constantly on edge, waiting for something else to happen to her at any time, knowing that I would have to react on my own—I had no help. I needed my husband to talk to—my partner—but we just couldn't connect. Soon, I couldn't remember the last time we were really connected and committed to each other. I couldn't even remember the last time it felt like we loved each other. Most of all, I needed Mike to give me hope for our family's future, but I wasn't sure he *had* hope— either for Nicki or for us. I found myself longing for his affection and some gesture of compassion, but it wasn't there: he was in his own world, and I was in mine. At times, I wondered if he felt the same way as I did. I wondered if maybe he wasn't attracted to me anymore. I never felt romantic anymore, and certainly didn't feel like having sex—which I thought was important to help men feel connected to their wives. Had I caused the separation? Was I the one who had first turned away from him? If that was the case, I wished he'd just come to me and tell me he loved me, and that he needed me too, but in the end he never did. As I didn't want Nicki to know how scared I was, I tried to keep upbeat around her. I especially didn't want her to feel that her disease had caused Mike and I to become separated, even if it did. But Nicki was so perceptive—she knew what was going on. I didn't know what to do; everything was so miserable and confusing.

During and after her radiation treatments, Nicki was still required to undergo chemotherapy every three weeks—and she would for the next three years. But a few weeks after she completed the radiation treatments, her headaches and vomiting returned, and we discovered that her brain had started to swell again. Dr. Nancy and I were in constant contact because everyone was so concerned about these side effects of radiation, so we met with Nicki's team of doctors and talked about what to do right away. First, they wanted us to bring her back to Shands for more tests; then, we needed to increase her steroids to keep the swelling in her brain down. Nicki hated this because the steroids made her body swell and caused weight gain— something that no teenage girl wants. All I could wonder was when this was going to start getting better. Once we were back at the hospital, Nicki's radiologist and neurosurgeon decided it was critical that she have surgery again, this time to remove some of the tumor, feeling that she would not survive without the surgery—the swelling was just too severe, and even though surgery would be dangerous, it was her only hope right now: we had no other option. What a trade-off: without the surgery, she could die; but, the surgery could kill her.

On the day of her surgery, Nicki remained positive as usual, and managed to flash a thumbs-up as they once again wheeled her away for her surgery. During the operation, Mike, Jesse, and I sat in an empty waiting room, each in our separate space, consumed by our own thoughts. Thankfully, one of Jesse's friends from Jacksonville came to be with him, which helped me relax a little more without having to worry about him so much. I spent the whole time praying that Nicki would make it. I asked God to give her surgeon comfort and peace, and to guide his hands through this long, tedious procedure. Twelve hours later, when her doctor finally came into the waiting room to talk to us, we were all exhausted. The surgeon looked weary too, and his once-clean and crisp scrubs were now wrinkled and blood-splattered. He spoke to us seriously, expressing his confidence that this delicate procedure had been successful; he had been able to remove as much of the tumor as he could without causing significant damage to her mentally or physically. He warned us, though, that part of the removal would cause her to lose peripheral vision in her right eye. And, to my dismay, he reminded us that this surgery would not save her life, though it would possibly give us another year with her.

I was overwhelmed with sadness, because I was still holding on to hope for a miracle that God would heal her completely, and that I would have a lifetime with her. But for now, Nicki was alive. We thanked the surgeon for his work, and I gave him a heartfelt hug, once again thanking God that she had cleared this hurdle. At the time, I had no idea that this was only one of many hurdles Nicki would jump over during the next two years.

A few days after her surgery Nicki was released from the hospital, and we were all happy to be headed home to Jacksonville once again. Jesse returned to Miami, relieved that his sister had made it through this dangerous procedure, but apprehensive to leave her again. Jesse's departures were always bittersweet, and I always felt sad to see him go, but he needed to go back to college to get on with his life, and he managed to call Nicki every day to check in. I was sorry, though: I wanted so much to talk to Jesse about school and ask how he and his girlfriend Kathy were doing. We hadn't talked in so long, since I was consumed with Nicki and wondering how I could ever survive losing her.

Thankful that she had once again survived surgery, and optimistic for her recovery, I couldn't wait to have Nicki back home this time. But as we tried to get on with our lives, we noticed that, this time, Nicki wasn't regaining her strength. Instead, she seemed to be getting weaker. Once more, her headaches returned, and this time they were extremely severe, and we knew the worst had happened: her brain was swelling from the surgery. We rushed her to the Children's Hospital again, where Nicki was quarantined in a sterile room while Mike and I waited for her examination. While we were waiting for the doctor, a nurse asked us the usual intake questions, and as she did, suddenly Nicki's arms and legs began to hyperextend, becoming stiff and rigid; her body jerked uncontrollably, her arms now rotating stiffly with her palms facing up. I didn't know what to do—I cried and left the room as the nurse called for help, bringing doctors and hospital personnel running into the room.

Now what? I thought. I sat alone on the floor outside the examining room while everyone tended to Nicki. It was total chaos and confusion. Finally one of the nurses came to tell me that Nicki needed to be intubated, and would be sent to intensive care immediately. While they took Nicki away, Mike and I were escorted to another room: a hospice representative wanted to speak with us. Without much ado, we were told to say good-bye to Nicki; a doctor, one we didn't recognize at all, warned us that Nicki most likely wouldn't make it out of the hospital alive. I was so stunned and hurt that I didn't even bother asking who he was.

Everything was spinning out of control.

We called Jesse yet again, and he drove as fast as he could from Miami to be with us. The three of us slept in Nicki's hospital room, trying to get comfortable on a long, built-in ledge running the length of the wall, though the lights in the ICU were always on and we slept in our clothes. Nurses were in and out of Nicki's room all night long, and though they offered me anti-anxiety medication, I refused—I'd never taken any before, and didn't want to start then. I hated to see Jesse living out of his duffel bag, overflowing with dirty clothes and unopened schoolbooks. I wanted to spend quality time with my son, but how could I when we were told my daughter was dying? We had nothing to talk about other than her. I was consumed with my daughter, and constantly prayed that she would live. And Mike and I just went through the motions together—I didn't feel connected to him at all anymore.

In all, we spent ten days in agony watching Nicki with that horrible plastic tube going into her trachea, surrounded by all those other tubes and monitors she was hooked up to. She just lay there, motionless and silent, breathing through the endotracheal tube. She was also using a ventilator to assist her breathing since we didn't know if she would be able to breathe on her own if they took the tubes out. The doctors had told us that Nicki was going to die any day now, and because of that we couldn't sleep for fear that she might be gone when we woke. During this time our family and friends came to see Nicki to say good-bye. Jesse had recently joined the Orthodox Church, and he was very fond of the church's pastor, Father Ted, who came immediately when he heard the news. I think it helped Jesse a lot to have Father Ted come to baptize and perform chrismation on Nicki. Chrismation is similar to confirmation in that Nicki had now received "the seal and the gift of the Holy Spirit," meaning that the Holy Spirit had now come upon her, adorning her with growth and strength in her spiritual life. Father Ted came every day to bless Nicki, which was such a comfort and blessing for our family. But it was so hard to see her like this, not knowing if we had truly lost her or not. I couldn't bear to see her there, so close to death. It made me sick.

During this time, February 14 rolled around, which was my twenty-second wedding anniversary with Mike. We were still in the hospital, but tried to celebrate; we sent Jesse out to pick up steaks, and we all silently ate from our Styrofoam containers in one of the private rooms on the ICU floor. I couldn't help but think back to our wedding in 1982, when Mike and I married right after he graduated from college. My dad had just died recently and I was grieving; we had only known each other about six months. And we were only married for a short time when Mike won the NCAA 1982 men's singles title, beating twelve-year professional Brad Gilbert in the finals. He became a mini celebrity after his NCAA win, with endorsements and invitations to major tournaments as just a few of the perks for his victory title. Soon he was given wild cards to compete in the Australian Open, French Open, Wimbledon, and the U.S. Open. I had quit my job as a hairdresser to travel with Mike to Hong Kong, Japan, China, France, Italy, Sweden, Australia, Germany, and London, a grueling schedule that kept us on the road most of the year. All of

Mike's time was spent competing, practicing for a match, eating, or sleeping, while I had to schedule my life—and eventually the kids' lives—around his tennis career. I tried to support him, but I was often homesick, missing my family and friends and the support that they gave me. I missed the empowerment of working, and I often felt isolated. But I was married now, and I wanted to support my husband and longed for our marriage to work, though it wasn't easy, because I loved him.

But now, twenty-two years later, as we sat together in a hospital room in an ICU with our teenage daughter, we were worlds away from the tennis tour. Our daughter was fighting for her life. Our son, who had made us so proud, was suffering the pain of possibly losing his only sibling while his parents were now divided. Above all, I felt that my husband and I were moving in different directions in terms of how we thought about Nicki's outcome: Mike was looking at the reality of it all, but I wanted to remain hopeful. And, I was beginning to slide into denial. But I *had* to believe that she would survive, and I wasn't about to ever give up—not then—not ever. Nothing would ever cause me to give up on my miracle. I refused to lose hope.

One afternoon, a few days after our anniversary, Mike and I were sitting outside of Nicki's hospital room. We sat side by side, leaning against the wall, cold, stunned, and devastated from all that was happening to us. Every day we were beaten down with statistics and medical reports from doctors who had witnessed this disease before. They gave us no hope.

I turned to my husband; I was desperate and pleading with him. "We're bound together forever now, because of this. We have to stay together."

I was ready to put some effort into saving our marriage; I couldn't imagine losing Mike. I wanted us to be close again. I reached over and placed my hand on his leg, but when I did he just sat there cold, staring into space. He said nothing. This was my fear: rejection. I couldn't take it—this was more pain than I could bear now.

And yet, I had finally faced my fear and had an answer: I was going to endure this unbearable pain alone. Mike had checked out. We'd always had our differences in our marriage, and there had been times when I had wondered if we wouldn't be better off not married to each other, but this hadn't been one of those times. Even though it was hard for me to meet his needs during this critical time, I needed my husband now. Jesse needed both of his parents. Without Mike and I, Jesse would endure this all alone too; I didn't want that for him. We were losing one child—I would do anything to make sure that I didn't lose Jesse too.

I thought back to a morning a few days after Nicki's surgery. Mike had been standing in our kitchen, decked out in brand-name tennis apparel: a new crisp, clean tennis shirt, tennis shorts, and a new pair of tennis shoes. Sports companies always sent him free clothes to wear for sponsorship purposes, so Mike had always looked sharp and professional. On that day, it should have been a usual morning, but we knew that nothing would ever be normal in our lives again. Before he walked out the door, we stood facing one another on opposite sides of the kitchen counter. My lips began to quiver as I tried to talk with him, but in a moment I broke down and began to cry. Trying to communicate with him was more than I could bear. The rejection was killing me, and I already felt beaten down enough from everything happening to Nicki. I knew that I was losing him and I just didn't have the energy to fix it by myself. He had to meet me halfway. Before he left, I managed to talk briefly. "Mike," I said, "it's important that we have each other to lean on through this. We need each other, if only for our children." He didn't even look at me—he just proceeded out the door, even though he knew my heart was breaking. I didn't want to endure this kind of pain alone, and felt that if I lost Nicki, I couldn't handle losing him too. Even as I felt us drift further apart, this was all I could think about.

So there we were, eight days later, still waiting on pins and needles, delirious from sleep deprivation, thinking that our little actress—our baby girl, our Nickster—was going to pass away, but nothing was happening. On the tenth day, the doctors felt it was time to remove the trachea tube, which they believed was the only thing keeping her alive. They told us that when they took the tube out of her throat we might only have about twenty minutes to say good-bye to her. We couldn't believe it had come to this; we went into to the hall to talk it over together. There we were, huddled together crying, hugging, and whispering. We had to make a decision right there, right then, about whether we wanted to keep her intubated longer or not. But though we were afraid, we knew that she couldn't go on like this. We felt that since she had remained stable, the doctor could remove the tubes: we had been watching Nicki very closely these past ten days, of course, and we all honestly believed that she would live. I couldn't believe that God would take her from me, because this was part of my miracle.

So I wasn't surprised when the doctor removed the tubes and Nicki opened her eyes, saying, "What's going on?" It was truly that amazing! Hallelujah! Praise the Lord!

I had finally gotten my miracle!

"I'm hungry. Can I have something to eat?" she continued. Nicki was calm, cool, and collected—and hungry! We, on the other hand, had been on an emotional roller coaster after just making the most gut-wrenching decision of our lives. When we told her that she had been unconscious for ten days, she was shocked. I asked Nicki if she thought she'd had an out-of-body experience, but she said no, that she didn't remember anything. She had no idea how much time had passed or what had happened, which I believed meant she hadn't been near death at all. Sometimes, the doctors just don't know.

Finally, we could pack up and go home. As Jesse began stuffing his clothes into his duffle bag, he turned to Nicki, who was watching him from her hospital bed. He asked her, "Ready to go home, Nickster?"

She gave him a sly smile, and in an upbeat voice answered, "Yes I am, Jesse. I'm ready to party."

We all laughed. It was great to see her sense of humor again. We were all exhausted, completely drained, but happy that we were finally going home: that's all that mattered.

Nicki's doctors weren't quite convinced that all was well though, so they ordered a hospital bed, a walker, and morphine patches to be sent home with us—they still thought she might not make it. When the hospital van pulled up in front of our house to deliver everything, it was depressing; it almost seemed like a very old person lived in our home, but instead it was all for a seventeen-year-old. That's really what made it all so hard: the reality of what our teenage daughter had become. Nicki didn't want any of it, and refused to use it. She was walking fine, so she didn't need the walker. We did put the hospital bed in our bedroom for two nights just to monitor her, but she was sleeping so well and wanted to sleep in her own bed that we finally called the hospital and sent everything back. Her doctors asked her to wear the morphine patches for a few days—just in case—so we followed doctors' orders and she wore them for a few days. They had to be taken away slowly, but Nicki seemed to be recovering quickly and started to get stronger and better every day, so within a week she stopped using the patches. We almost couldn't believe how soon she was improving after this devastating experience. For my part, I just continued to thank God daily for answering my prayers.

At this point, Jesse had missed a huge amount of time in college in Miami, and after this emotional week in the ICU he made the decision to move back to Jacksonville, which frankly made me happy. Knowing the severity of Nicki's condition, he wanted to be close to his sister and spend as much time with her as he could. At the same time, though, by enrolling at the University of North Florida, here in Jacksonville, he not only gave up his scholarship to the University of Miami, but for some reason he stopped playing his guitar. The University of Miami held his scholarship for one year, hoping things would get better so that Jesse would come back, but in the end it wasn't meant to be.

Although Nicki began to improve, she wasn't quite ready to go back to school, and she was very concerned about falling behind. So, she began studying through a program called Hospital Homebound, in which she took classes over the telephone, with other students and a teacher together on the line. I sometimes wondered if any of the other students had a medical condition that affected their brains like Nicki. Nicki's classes were in the morning, scheduled at different times. When she got up, she would bring her books to the dining room table and put on a telephone headset, so her hands were free to write. Then she would call into her class, where a teacher and other students were all connected. She absolutely *hated* this, and so did I.

One morning I got up late and found Nicki already sitting at the table; she was wearing her purple and gray Eeyore pajama bottoms rolled down around her hips, a pink tank top, and had her hair twisted in a messy bun on top of her head: her usual look when she was lounging around the house or doing homework late at night. But then I noticed that, this morning, she was crying.

"What's wrong, honey?" I asked, concerned.

"Mommy, I can't learn this way. I'm a visual person—this is so confusing," she said, sobbing.

This way of learning was obviously not going to work for Nicki. It was only her second week into this new program, and she was trying so hard, but it just wasn't getting better. It was miserable watching her struggle to understand what was expected of her, but due to all the radiation and chemotherapy, her brain was behaving differently than a normal brain. And, as she was naturally a visual and social person, this style of learning didn't fit her at all. Throughout everything, she never wanted me to interfere and always tried to be as independent as possible, doing everything on her own that she could, so I had tried to observe from close range. But this was different: I needed to help her do something about this situation, immediately. I contacted her guidance counselor, Kathy Mortenson, at DASOTA, who was more than understanding, and arranged to have Nicki's work sent home to her every day. This was a huge relief for Nicki, and since her goal was to go back to school as soon as possible, we felt comfortable that, this way, when she was ready to return, she would be able to keep up with her classmates. Ms. Mortenson was wonderful and always made sure Nicki got her work assignments on time so that she wouldn't fall behind.

I was trying to keep Nicki's life as normal as I could, but it was a challenge. Her friends were social, driving around, involved in school activities, and all currently applying to their dream colleges. It was natural that they couldn't understand what Nicki was going through, but that worried me. How could they relate? They were teenagers, and Nicki's daily routine no longer included most of the things that her friends were doing. She wasn't in charge of her day anymore—her disease was. Even I wouldn't have really understood this if I hadn't been spending 24/7 with her, watching her life first-hand. Nothing was more painful than watching my normally happy, outgoing, intelligent child become isolated from school and friends.

Watching her deal with emotional issues that came from having cancer was devastating, too. It had been a huge deal to Nicki that she could possibly lose her hair from treatments, and she had been unbelievably relieved when she found out that the type of chemo she would use wouldn't cause her hair to fall out. But we hadn't thought about how the radiation treatments could cause hair loss.

One day, while I was in the kitchen loading the dishwasher, I could hear Nicki in the shower. It always made me nervous when she took a shower because she locked the bathroom door and I worried that she might slip and fall and we wouldn't be able to open the door. These are the types of things that a mother of a seventeen-year-old usually doesn't ever think about, but I was so protective of her. I always asked her to please leave the door unlocked, but she refused. "Mommy, what are you worried about?" she'd say. "Please *stop*." So I tried to let it go. But today was different. The shower stopped; Nicki walked into the kitchen with a towel wrapped around her body, her hair soaking wet and dripping onto the floor. She held out her hand, and I saw that she was holding a clump of her long, blond hair. Her eyes were swollen and red, tears falling down her face. I was at a loss for words, and so I wrapped her in my amrs and held her as she sobbed. She had just wanted to be able to blend in with everyone else; losing her hair, such a visible symptom, was her biggest fear.

At one of her follow-up appointments, her neurologist decided to put her on an anti-seizure medication, and I questioned why it was necessary—since she had never had a seizure, I worried that they wanted to put her on another medication. Her doctor explained to me that because her brain was compromised, she was now very susceptible to having one. And, sure enough, one day it happened and scared the living daylights out of me.

We were all at home relaxing; Nicki was sitting in her favorite spot, a recliner chair with a table that folded down where she could put her cell phone, school books, snacks, and whatever else she wanted beside her. I was in the kitchen, talking back and forth, but now I noticed that she had suddenly become very quiet, which seemed strange. I tried to continue our conversation, but she just stared into space, which really scared me. I've come to know now that these were two of the major signs of an impending seizure—sudden silence; staring into space—but at the moment I was scared and confused. I went into the family room and stood right in front of her, blocking the TV, and asked her if she was okay, hoping to get an answer, but Nicki just stared right through me. Then suddenly she moaned loudly, her body becoming stiff for a moment and then jerking wildly. Her eyes were blinking and fluttering.

I was terrified to touch her, and had no clue what to do. Her doctors hadn't explained what to do if she should have a seizure, and I was so scared that I panicked. I called Mike at work, crying hysterically into the phone. He raced home immediately, and when he arrived she was still seizing, her body rigid and jerking; she was chewing her tongue. We thought that we should rush her to the hospital, so her dad picked her up, while her body jerked like a bunking bronco, and carried her to my car, laying her gently in the backseat. She seized the whole time we drove to the hospital. I felt *helpless*. I couldn't believe how many horrible situations I now found myself in, with no idea at the time how to handle them without calling for help. I was so afraid that if I did something wrong, I would hurt her or make the situation worse. Later, I learned that I should have not moved Nicki, and should have just let the seizure happen, simply watching her closely and placing a pillow under her head to ensure that she didn't accidentally hurt herself. In fact, when we arrived at the hospital, the doctors didn't need to do much since she came out of the seizure herself, and seemed all right. But Nicki had chewed her tongue so badly that she had to sip liquid food through a straw for two weeks, which made me feel horrible because I thought I might have prevented that from happening if I had only known what to do.

From then on, Nicki's medicine was increased, and her doctor began to alter her anti-seizure medication, changing it dozens of times before finding the right one for her. I learned that there are hundreds of anti-seizure medications, and, unfortunately, all of them have potential side effects. A few months after that incident, she was hospitalized once again since her seizure medication caused her potassium to drop too low—which caused a seizure. Go figure. The number of pills Nicki had to take kept increasing, so I finally went and got pill containers to keep track of them all. A couple of these medications required us to get up twice during the night; we even had to designate one of our kitchen cabinets to hold all of the pills, there were so many. Some of her medications were steroids, seizure medication, chemotherapy, various pain medications, stomach medication, and anti-nausea pills. It broke my heart to watch my child take so much medication. And, as if that weren't difficult enough, she needed to go to the clinic for weekly respiratory breathing treatments, blood work, and a monthly MRI.

This was by far the hardest year for Nicki. One day she said, "This is a bad age to get cancer, Mommy. I feel like if this had happened to me when I was a little girl, it would have been easier to handle. Little kids are used to hanging out with their moms. I was looking forward to applying to colleges and being on my own now."

I just looked at her, then dropped my head. What could I say? Pediatric hospitals and clinics are decorated with images of clowns and red wagons for young children—they aren't places for teenagers or young adults. Although Nicki's heart ached when she saw the little kids with cancer, she felt totally isolated during this time. She just wanted to be with her friends, peers her own age. This was the time when children turn into young adults, get jobs, drive cars, learn who they are, and finally start achieving their goals. Instead, Nicki was realizing that the hopes and dreams that she had planned for were probably never going to happen for her now. When Nicki was given one to three years to live, she knew that the rest of her time would be spent fighting cancer. She knew there would be no trips, no travel, no jobs or work or vacations. She needed to be close to home for her treatments. Survival was her only goal these days.

This had been another really tough year; we all felt beaten down. It was at this point that I asked God for three specific things. I asked that Nicki be able to return to school for her senior year, that she could go to her prom, and that she could walk with her class at graduation. Although her friends from school still called her, they were busy with their lives, and it hurt me to see Nicki left behind. Fortunately, she had three very close friends who always went above and beyond to let her know that they cared. One of them, Jordan, had met Nicki when she was eight years old. Jordan was our neighbor, living right down the street from ours. Growing up, Nicki and Jordy spent almost every day together, mostly at our house, since both of Jordan's parents worked, and I was a stay-at-home mom who could supervise. They played everything together, from dress-up to Barbies, board games, and kick-the-can. I remember how Nicki comforted Jordy the day she came over crying because her parents had announced that they would be getting divorced and she might be moving out of our neighborhood. They had always relied on each other, and when Nicki got sick, Jordy was there for her too: just as Nicki had taken care of her, now Jordy came over almost every day to comfort her.

Another friend, Katie, met Nicki in middle school, where they quickly found out that they had a lot in common. Since both of them only had brothers, they shared a special "sister" bond as well as a passion for acting, singing, and performing; they even performed in a singing group together. It didn't take long before they were best friends. Katie nicknamed Nicki "Binky." During middle school the girls spent every weekend together, with at least one night at each other's house. Everyone knew that Nicki and Katie were best friends and would stay that way forever. The summer before their junior year of high school, Katie found out that she had been accepted into a theater school in North Carolina. Before applying to that school, Katie had hoped that Nicki would go with her, but Nicki was set on going to DASOTA. She knew she would miss Katie dearly, but she also was confident that nothing would ever come between them. Even though they weren't together in person anymore, they talked on the phone every day and stayed close. Katie loved Nicki, and came home whenever she could on the weekends to be with her. When we called Katie to tell her that Nicki had a brain tumor, she was horrified, and rushed back as fast as she could to be by Nicki's side for the surgery. Over time, Katie made many more trips back to Jacksonville during Nicki's illness to spend time with her "Binky," picking her up to go shopping and to have lunch and dinner together. The last time Katie came over to pick Nicki up and take her out, I watched them leave the house, all dressed up and eager to go like old times, and was heartbroken to see such a huge difference between the girls now: Katie looked so healthy and vibrant, and Nicki looked so weak and tired. But Katie was truly amazing, protecting Nicki like a big sister and yet still treating her like nothing had ever changed.

Nicki met her friend Ryan on the first day of their freshmen year at DASOTA. He called her "Nick Nick," and from that day on, he became a constant in her life. Ryan lived just a mile from our house, so he spent almost every day with Nicki. They never actually dated, but were very close friends—so much so that everyone always wondered if they were dating. She even took family vacations with Ryan and his parents. "Nick Nick" was part of their family. The summer before their junior year, right before Nicki got sick, Ryan's dad got transferred to California to start a new job, which was devastating for Nicki. I wondered how they would survive without each other; the timing seemed terrible. But I knew that they loved each other and that they would eventually find a way to work it out and be together. After Nicki was diagnosed, Ryan couldn't stay away from her and flew back to be with his "Nick Nick," even driving her to doctor appointments and accompanying her to Shands for radiation treatments. Although Ryan wasn't able to be with her all of the time, he would call her every morning and every evening from California. He loved Nicki from the bottom of his heart, and once told me, "I don't think I will ever feel that way about anyone ever again."

SERENITY

Summer brought sunshine and, with it, a ray of hope, and things finally started to look up. Nicki continued to improve, although we all knew that she was not out of the woods just yet. Because Ms. Mortenson had sent her assignments home daily during her junior year, and since Nicki was naturally so bright, by August she was ready to start her senior year of school. We had decreased the amount of steroids she had been taking and her weight was back to normal, so off to the mall we went for new clothes! Nicki's favorite attire was mostly blue jeans and simple T-shirts or tank tops, and it had been a while since she could fit into her size-two jeans, but now that she had lost the weight from the steroids she was excited to buy new clothes. I wanted this to be a fresh start, so I encouraged her to take as much as she could into the dressing room to try on. As I waited in the dressing room, watching her try on jeans and tops, I couldn't help but notice how she examined her body in the mirror, twisting and turning to see her backside in the mirror behind her. I could tell that she was pleased with the way she looked. It had been a rough year with all the hospitalizations, medications, and body changes, and I was glad that we were able to finally have such a fun day shopping for new school clothes. After a long day, Nicki walked happily out of the store carrying a full bag of her favorite things, while I walked behind her, smiling because I felt that now, after so much, she was going to be okay.

Although Nicki was apprehensive about going back to school, since she would be together with her friends on a daily basis now, I could stop worrying about her being isolated. She had so many great friends at DASOTA who were anxiously awaiting her return, and I figured that she would do just fine. So on that first day, while she was sitting on the couch waiting for her ride to come, I couldn't help but look at my daughter with admiration. She was wearing her new size-two jeans, a simple green shirt, white sneakers, and flowered purple socks. Her silky blonde hair, which now looked healthy, was pulled back in a high ponytail. She looked good! Unless you knew her, there was no telltale sign that she had cancer. When her friends pulled up in the driveway, she jumped off the couch, grabbed her book bag, then turned to me with a sweet smile and said, "I'll be okay, Mommy. Please, don't worry." Once again she reminded me just how much determination to continue on with her life she had, even while her life had changed by leaps and bounds in the past year as her classmates' lives had pretty much remained the same. She would still have to adjust to some things, but we all knew that Nicki was no quitter.

Her first week back, Dr. Beger happily informed Nicki that she would be teaching acting to some of the incoming freshmen. She was so excited about the responsibility, and I was very thankful that Dr. Beger gave her that opportunity. Then, another day, Nicki came home and told me that she would be performing in one of the school's musical productions; I hugged her so hard, I think I almost broke her back! Glory, glory, she was back in her element! I thanked God for the progress she was making and for answering my prayers, and every day kept praying that she would make it all the way through her senior year and be able to graduate with her class.

At this point, Nicki was required to have an MRI every three months, and the latest showed that the tumor was not growing; and, she didn't need the steroids anymore because her brain was no longer swelling. This was *huge* for Nicki: she was finally at her normal weight, and she wanted to stay there—besides, she hated taking the steroids. We knew that, with this disease, everything wasn't perfect, and we were used to things changing overnight, but now we chose to cautiously look forward to the future. We were thankful for every day with her. Nicki was still required to have chemotherapy every three weeks as a precaution to keep the tumor from growing, and that made her tired, and gave her some short-term memory and slight cognitive problems. Yet even with all of this, and what she had already been through, Nicki still continued to maintain an amazing attitude; she never let anything that happened to her get in the way of moving on with her life. I looked at my daughter with such admiration, every day, and knew that Nicki had become my role model.

Since she was doing so much better and hadn't had a seizure in over six months, her neurologist agreed to slowly wean her off the anti-seizure medicine—having watched her suffer such serious side effects from all her medications, her doctors and I always tried to reduce or eliminate any that she might not need. Her dose had already been decreased to half its normal amount, and we knew from the MRI reports that the tumor was stable, so I thought that she might not need them anymore. Anytime Nicki had a medication change, I was extra careful, knowing anything could go wrong without warning. So, I began driving her to and from school—which was not exactly what she wanted, since all of the other seniors were driving themselves, but she never showed it, instead thanking me repeatedly for it.

On one particular day, though, I noticed that she seemed different; she was unusually quiet. I knew from past experiences that this wasn't good: it wasn't Nicki's personality to be *so* quiet unless something was wrong. But, of course, the problem with this disease was that, with so many things that *could* be going on, it was sometimes hard to determine if something was a symptom. She could have just been tired that day—and I hoped that was all it was. I suggested that she stay home from school, but I knew she didn't want another day home with Mom: she wanted to go to school and stay after for play rehearsal. So, I drove her to school and dropped her off. After all, she was eighteen now. She had been fighting for her life for over a year now, and I felt that she would be safe if anything did happen. Everyone at her high school had been very supportive and was willing to do anything they could to help her or our family through this heartbreaking situation. And, above all, we wanted her to be able to live her life as normally as possible. I tried not to treat her differently, and to support her decisions, since it bothered her when I became overprotective, but it was so hard not to be.

But, I always had my phone with me just in case—and when it rang at five o'clock that afternoon, I knew something had happened to her. Sure enough, it was Dr. Beger calling to tell me that Nicki had a seizure during play rehearsal; they'd called 911, and Nicki was being taken to the hospital by ambulance. I immediately called Mike; we drove downtown to the Childrens' Hospital where we found her in the ER—dressed in costume as a pioneer, in a long brown homespun skirt with a crisp white apron tied around her waist. She had a ruffled bonnet tied in a big bow around her neck, which made her look about twelve years old: the disease sometimes caused her to look younger. While we waited, I watched as she entertained the doctors and nurses. This, in particular, is such a special memory because, as always, Nicki was able to turn a bad situation into something positive. I miss that about her so much.

Before we left to go home, the doctors told us she needed to increase her seizure medication again. We had hoped that she wouldn't have another incident like this, but knew it could happen. On the ride home, Nicki was upbeat, telling us about play rehearsal and what she remembered before she had the seizure. This had become normal life for our family: living on the edge, knowing that anything could happen at any time. We all knew that Nicki's disease controlled our lives.

CHRISTMAS 2004

Nicki had always been fascinated by photography, so for Christmas her paternal grandparents from Boston gave her a professional camera. At the time, of course, we didn't know that it would be her last Christmas with us—only that Nicki adored her camera, playing with it and buying books on photography, sophisticated lenses, and a tripod. I loved watching how the camera became her constant companion, as it would be for the remainder of her life. She found great comfort in the camera, and took many beautiful photos of the beach, trees, insects, roads, paths, and sunsets—anything in the great outdoors. Nicki always had to have a passion for something, and since her diagnosis her goals had changed; acting and performing had become too much of a challenge for her, and with the realization that she wouldn't be able to do it much anymore, she switched gears. But that's what we all loved about her: she always managed to find peace and meaning in her life, no matter what she was going through. As time went on, Nicki was even more determined that, if cancer was inevitably going to take some things from her, it wasn't going to steal her joy. I was glad to see that her camera gave her something to do full of joy and peace. Nicki was a visual person and loved to create things, but even more than that, she loved to give creative gifts to others; her photography, in that way, was a gift.

Nicki loved turtles, and we had a lot of large ones in the local ponds and lakes. Early one morning, when she had just gotten up, still in her pajamas, she spotted an enormous turtle in our backyard. She quickly grabbed her camera, and out the door she went! Of course, when she approached the turtle to take its picture, the turtle immediately hid its head in its protective shell. But Nicki really wanted a picture of the turtle's face, so she was very persistent. Incidentally, turtles have very good eyesight— they see in color—and I think this turtle might have noticed how pretty she was and gotten shy! After a minute or two, the turtle turned tail and began to hobble away from her. Nicki, though, just patiently followed it through the whole neighborhood, not at all concerned that she was in her pajamas. She was determined to get a good photo, and wasn't about to give up until she got the perfect shot.

I remember watching her follow that turtle all the way down the street: she would walk, then pause and stand there very still, waiting, her camera aimed at the turtle. She looked so comfortable, even in bare feet, her pajama, and with messy bed-head hair. Nicki wasn't concerned with the way she looked anymore; now, a true photographer, her only desire was to get the picture. Although she was still fighting her battle with cancer, she was determined that this photograph of the turtle was a task that she would win. Almost a full hour passed before the turtle finally succumbed to her persistent desire: sure enough, the turtle carefully poked his face out and ever so slowly stretched his long neck, looking directly into the camera lens. It was as if the turtle knew Nicki was special, and he was saying to her, "Okay, are you happy now?" After she took the turtle's photo, I watched Nicki run back to the house, her camera strapped around her neck, both hands holding the lens so it wouldn't move. Her smile was huge. She hadn't seen me watching from the window, admiring how long she stayed focused. My daughter was constantly reaffirming her strength, showing me that she was a fighter who never gave up—and in turn that gave *me* strength. I was amazed at how much I was learning from her.

School continued to go well for Nicki, but I knew that it was taxing on her and she needed a break. So, when spring break rolled around, Nicki's friend Katie announced she was coming back to Jacksonville to spend her vacation with Nicki; the girls were ecstatic to spend their time together, and I was relieved and happy that Nicki would see her friend. Once Katie got home, they went somewhere different every day for lunch, and in the evening they would go out again to the movies or to clubs to dance. Seeing them together every day, so happy, was a blessing. And, at the same time, Jesse took Nicki out with him too. They would go to his favorite clubs, or drive down to St. Augustine to meet friends and listen to bands, or go to the movies, or just hang out at a friend's house and have a barbeque. We were all so glad that Nicki was finally back to living her life in a more normal way.

Since God had answered my first prayer that Nicki would be able to go back to school, I was praying hard for my second request: that Nicki would get asked to her senior prom. And, it didn't take God long to respond: soon enough, Nicki's friend Ryan, knowing that she was doing well, called her up and told her to pick out a dress because he was going to fly in from California to take his "Nick Nick" to her senior prom. He didn't even have to ask her— they both knew it was meant to be that they would go together. Nicki and I immediately went looking for the perfect prom dress. As I waited in several store dressing rooms while Nicki tried on elegant dresses, I looked at how beautiful she was and tried not to break down as I imagined us one day looking for her wedding.

When Ryan flew in from Los Angeles, we met him at the airport. He and Nicki ran to meet each other, hugged, and immediately started being silly, laughing together. It seemed just like old times. Once back at our house, Ryan dropped his bags in Jesse's room, and Nicki went and grabbed her dress to show him. It was a short, bright-coral chiffon Marilyn Monroe-style dress with a halter top that tied in a bow around her neck. The fitted waist and bare back showed off her beautiful figure. On prom night, Nicki wore her hair in a ponytail, with her long bangs swept over to the side. Her coral and pearl earrings dangled on her neck, and her makeup was soft and natural. I thought she looked like a Broadway star. To match her, Ryan wore a coral tie with his tuxedo. Together, they looked stunning. They could have walked the red carpet hand-in-hand that evening!

Right before they left the house, Ryan slipped a delicate white corsage on her wrist. Nicki motioned for me to get Ryan's coral boutonniere, and when I handed it to her, she carefully pinned the flower on his lapel, chuckling the whole time. We took so many pictures before they left the house, knowing that these photos would be cherished forever. As they walked out the door, Ryan already had Nicki laughing. I went inside to my bedroom, lay across my king-size bed, folded my hands, and said, "Thank you, God!"

Ryan and Nicki stayed out until four in the morning, but I wasn't concerned. I was totally at peace, knowing how important this night was for her.

After the prom, all of Nicki's classmates were getting excited to go off to their dream college the next autumn. I knew it would be hard on Nicki, watching all their excitement, but I also knew that she was thankful that she, too, would be able to go to college, even if it was the University of North Florida, a local university just five miles from our home. So far, God had been faithful in answering my prayers, and I was overjoyed that He answered my third prayer request: that spring, Nicki walked with her high school class for graduation. Even better, everyone in our family came together to be with Nicki that night. Her grandparents from Boston were there, as well as my parents from Fort Myers, my sister and her two daughters from Michigan, my brother and his son, and Mike's siblings from Boston. The whole family was there to celebrate this milestone event with us; I was so happy we were all together.

During graduation, Nicki had been placed on the top row of the bleachers, which made me nervous—I kept wondering if she would be able to make it safely down the stairs. She was wearing heels, her balance wasn't very good anymore, and she had lost her peripheral vision in her right eye from surgery. Plus, the auditorium was dimly lit; what if she tripped and fell? I always had a hard time stepping back to let her live her life, since her limitations—that we knew about—weren't always visible. I was relieved when she made it safely to the stage and was handed her diploma. Everyone in the audience stood up and applauded her, and, in addition to her diploma, the high school awarded her a special plaque for her perseverance. After graduation, we took Nicki to her favorite restaurant to toast her achievement. Once again, we took tons of photos and had a never-to-be-forgotten evening. The next day, we had a party at our house; we served Nicki's favorite foods, topped off with a "2004 Graduation" cake, celebrating with family and all of Nicki's friends.

Now that Nicki had made it through high school and walked at graduation, I wanted her to be able to go to college. And, though I knew it wasn't prudent, I began to imagine beyond college to her wedding day and my future grandchildren. I had to tell myself stop, to take one day at a time, be thankful for every day. God had been gracious—I should be thankful for the blessings that He had already given us.

Nicki had a couple of months before she started college, and again I gave thanks that she could now rest and be able to sleep in, just doing what she wanted to do—even if it was nothing at all. But, I knew that wasn't really Nicki's style: even on days when she wasn't feeling well, she didn't want to sit around the house. Instead, she wanted to get out and *live*. Every day, she wanted to do as much as she could. It was a beautiful, hot summer, and Nicki and I began to take daily walks together. Experiencing the Atlantic Ocean, so close to our house that it felt like an afterthought, had never really been a priority in our lives, but now it seemed like it held magnetic powers that drew us close for comfort. Nicki would grab her camera, and on our half-mile walk to the beach along the Guana Preserve, she would photograph all the wildlife she saw: lizards, birds, ducks, caterpillars—she captured them all. When she went downtown for her clinic visits, she took her camera so that after her appointments we could walk along the St. Johns River, which flowed past the hospital, and she could take photos there too. We loved the skyline in downtown Jacksonville, with its many bridges, and Nicki liked to photograph it in the evening when the Florida sunsets would create a breathtaking landscape, with all the sunlight reflecting off the water.

I cherish all my daughter's photographs so much because they are originals, untouched impressions of Nicki's view. These treasures reflect the beauty she saw all around her as she battled something so ugly. I will always hold this time we spent together in my memory, just the two of us, as a gift, and I'll remember her senior year as the year that Nicki captured beautiful memories with her camera that will last my whole lifetime. So I always thank God for the photographs, and for allowing Nicki to discover and fulfill another passion in her life.

DENIAL

One warm summer evening, while out with friends, Nicki met a boy named Matt, whose band from Tampa was playing at a local club in Jacksonville. They caught each other's eye and talked all evening long, and at the end of the night, Nicki happily traded her phone number for one of the band's CDs. I found it fitting that his band was called "Ann Arbor," because Nicki had been born there. The next day, Matt called her; I could hear her laughing in her room while she talked, which made me smile. It had been a long time since someone new had brought laughter out of her like that. I had always thought that as soon as she got better and was able to go out more, she would attract someone special right away. This chance meeting with Matt was the start of a continued cell phone relationship that seemed to be growing stronger with every call. The next month, Matt's band came back to Jacksonville to play another gig, and Nicki went to see him again. All of her friends were so excited for her; just seeing her so happy, felt like the good old times. But little did we know that it would be short-lived.

As she and Matt continued to become more interested in each other, I started getting concerned: I knew that Nicki had not told Matt she had cancer. He lived far enough away that he couldn't see the daily grind of her day-to-day life, or understand what her life was even like. But I didn't want to interfere: after all, she was eighteen, and I didn't think it was the time for me to start getting involved in her relationships. I trusted Nicki's judgment, and had always left it up to her to make her own decision about these kinds of matters. I had been watching her make life-and-death choices every day, and knew that she would handle this in her own time, in her own way. While I could tell that Nicki was starting to have deeper feelings for Matt, and worried me, I knew I had to let go and give this one to God.

At some point, Nicki told me that she wanted to visit Matt in Tampa. I felt that it would be nice for her to get out of Jacksonville, but since she couldn't go on her own, we came up with a plan: I would go with her, and since I would want to have someone to hang out with while Nicki and Matt were visiting each other, we invited my friend Lorrie. Lorrie and I always spent a lot of time together, and Nicki often accompanied us to our favorite restaurants and movies. Nicki used to make fun of us because she thought it was funny at our age that we were always together. But she loved Lorrie, and of course I did, too. So—we had our plan in place, booked a hotel room for the weekend, and the three of us headed for Tampa. Yippee! We had so much fun that weekend, shopping at the mall, eating at new restaurants... and when we left Tampa, Nicki and Matt were on their cell phones, talking to each other the whole way home.

A few weeks after our Tampa trip, Nicki began her freshman year at the University of North Florida. She was so excited about a new beginning, and saw college as a fresh start. At this time, she was doing pretty well physically and was even able to drive herself to school. Through classes, she continued to make new friends, which I thought was so important; I loved hearing about all the new people in her life. But still, she had this hidden disease, cancer, hiding inside her brain. It was entirely Nicki's choice whether or not to tell anyone at UNF that she had cancer. In fact, it would have been hard to tell that she was battling cancer just by looking at her: the oral chemotherapy used to fight brain cancer doesn't necessarily cause a person to lose their hair like other chemotherapy drugs do, and although Nicki often looked thin and tired—as many college students do—how could anyone know that she had a stage-four malignant tumor in her brain? At one point radiation caused her to lose some of her hair, but it had all grown back by now. She was naturally beautiful, and there really were no obvious signs of what she was going through—which was exactly the way she wanted it.

Although she did well in her classes, it was a busy fall, so having some extra time off for the approaching Labor Day holiday was nice. Since we hadn't had a family photo taken in over three years, and Nicki was doing better than ever, I told my husband that I would like to have our family photographed on the beach to use for our Christmas cards. We hadn't been close for a long time, but we were still a *family*—and I needed this memory.

So on Thanksgiving Day 2004, I arranged for a professional photographer to take our family's photo. The Atlantic Ocean had become Nicki's source of peace, and now I wanted to capture what might be our final family photo in Nicki's favorite setting. As the four of us walked to the beach from our house, on that picture-perfect Florida day, we all knew this wasn't like previous holidays, and yet I was relieved that Nicki and Jesse seemed at ease, even though Mike and I didn't speak a word to each other the whole day. Once on the beach we met up with our photographer, just as the sun was setting. The sky was on fire with sunset colors as the four of us grouped together, all wearing matching blue jeans and white shirts; our background became a warm canvas of fiery orange, red, and golden hues. We stood together, our backs to the Atlantic Ocean, while a gentle breeze brushed against us and the sky cast a glow over the calm waters. With our arms wrapped around each other's waists, we captured our family memory—a beautiful moment in time.

When we were finished, I asked our photographer if he could take a photo of just Jesse and Nicki together; then, I asked to have a single picture of Nicki taken. She was barefoot in the sand, her hair gleaming gold in the sun, wearing a simple white V neck shirt. She stood with both thumbs tucked into the belt loops of her worn-out jeans, captivating the camera with her natural elegance. While looking at her on the beach that day, I could so clearly see her inner strength, and realized how resilient she had been while battling cancer. I was comforted by her smile, so soft and natural. She truly seemed at peace.

That December, just three weeks before Christmas, Mike called us into the family room of our home, as he had an announcement to make. It was there, gathered around him on our big La-Z Boy sectional, that he shocked us with the abrupt news that he would be moving out of the house on January 1. He didn't give us a reason, and we were all so dumbstruck that no one asked him why. I couldn't believe he hadn't spoken to me first about this. Although our marriage had been less than perfect over the years, and recently there had been more distance between us than usual, I was dumbfounded at his timing. How could he do this to me now, or to our kids? To *Nicki*, who was fighting for her life?

Mike told us that he would be moving just a mile away, in case we needed him; he wanted to stay close so that he could see Nicki every day. I saw a tear slip down Jesse's cheek as his dad delivered this staggering news. I could sense Jesse's fear, as he would now be the one who Nicki and I would rely on. Nicki sat on the couch hugging a pillow, showing no emotion at first. Although she didn't say a word, I could soon see it on her face: her heart was breaking. Though her two-year battle with cancer had slightly impaired her cognitive skills, she knew what her father's announcement meant for all of us. Not knowing the best way to react with both children there, I broke the awkward silence by suggesting that we go to counseling as a family; perhaps a counselor could help us all to work through what we were experiencing, in a space we would be able to talk about what was going on in our lives. However, Mike declined. When I heard that, I told myself not to panic; I didn't know how to react yet, and felt scared. I ached all over, especially for our children. I knew this would put a huge burden on all of us, especially Nicki—she was so vulnerable right now. How was I going to manage this alone?

Mike got up, went into our bedroom, and closed the door. Jesse went into his room, while Nicki turned to me and said, "Mommy I need to talk to Dad." I told her it was okay; she jumped off the couch and followed behind Jesse. She ran and knocked on our bedroom door and, with a trembling voice, I heard her say, "Dad, I need to talk to you." He opened the door, and she went in.

My heart was pounding as I went over to the closed bedroom door and stood listening from the outside. I could hear both of them sobbing as Nicki begged her father to stay. I wanted to open the door and grab her, but I had to let her do this. I was afraid that Mike would yell at me if I interfered, and that I would have made it worse for Nicki. Underneath the fear and panic, I was so furious at Mike—because of course I was extremely concerned for Nicki's mental state. This type of situation wasn't good at all for her. What was Mike's *problem*? How could he not know how bad it was for Nicki to be this upset?

I stood outside the door patiently waiting, and finally, when she came out, I took her into her room, closed the door, and she fell into my arms. Her father had made a firm decision, and even she couldn't persuade him to stay. I tried to assure her that we would be all right: I would be there, and Jesse would help us. But despite what I said, it seemed like things just kept getting harder and harder.

For the next three weeks, we still had to live with Mike in the house. Later, I found out that Mike had already purchased a condo before his announcement. At the time, I wasn't even concerned about the hows or whys—I was just glad that it was located close by so he could see Nicki every day. After he moved, Nicki and I only talked about his departure a single time. It was one day when we were sitting together on the couch watching TV. She looked over at me and said, "Mommy, it's okay that Dad left. He just couldn't handle it." I looked at her and nodded in agreement. What could I say? She continued: "Mommy, you've had a hard life. Your dad died of cancer when you

were young and now I have cancer, and your husband left."
I told her that I was all right, and that I just wanted her to
get better. She was always so concerned for me, and I knew
that she was worried about what would happen to me after
her dad moved out, but I also knew that she needed me to
be strong.

The day her dad packed up and left, Nicki took one look
at his empty walk-in closet and simply moved everything
from her closet into his—so she wouldn't be reminded of
his absence. Or maybe it was for me; maybe she thought it
would be hard for me to look at it empty every day. I don't
know for sure. She just filled it right up.

All the while, my heart felt like it was dying a slow,
agonizing death while I tried to keep my composure for her.
I was also concerned for all that Jesse would now be taking
on. I would need his help because Nicki often got sick in the
middle of the night and needed to be transported to the
hospital. Also, someone would have to be home with her at
all times because it would be dangerous for her to be left
alone in case of a seizure. If I needed to go out, Jesse would
now have to stay with Nicki, but he was trying to go to
school. I kept wondering, *Why does Mike have to leave
now?*

It was shortly after Mike moved out that things began
to rapidly go downhill for Nicki. Lately, she hadn't been
feeling well most of the time, so I had been driving for her.
She was so disappointed: Nicki had been given a car in April
of 2003 as a gift from three families in our community who
owned car dealerships. We had chosen Easter Sunday to
surprise her with it. I will never forget that day: we placed
a six-foot blow-up bunny holding a giant Easter basket on
the roof of her car. The bunny was adorned with heavy

makeup and wore a frilly dress, shiny red shoes, and a giant bow in its hair. That morning, when Nicki awoke, Mike, Jesse, and I walked her outside to our driveway where we'd parked the new car. Then we handed her the keys, and shouted, "Happy Easter, Nicki!" She was so overwhelmed, standing barefoot in her pajamas, that she covered her face with her hands and began sobbing. But she was so happy, and drove her very-own car to church that day to celebrate Easter.

But the next day she had a seizure, and her driving privileges were revoked. And now, as she started her second semester at UNF, she wasn't feeling well enough to drive—and worse, I had to drive her in her new car. It was bad enough in high school, but to have your mom drive you when you're in college? I felt so badly for her. We always parked in the very back of the university parking lot so that no one would see her getting out of the car with her mom. Poor Nicki—she had such a gentle spirit and was so attractive that boys were always interested in her, and would follow her out to the parking lot after class for the opportunity to talk to her. So, that was another reason why we parked in the back: to spare the explanation why her mother had to drive her. No one knew about her cancer.

It was now January, and classes had started again. That morning, I drove her car to the back of the lot to drop her off like I always did. But, when I turned to say good-bye, I noticed that she was shaking, shivering as if she were very cold. I panicked. "Nicki, honey, what's wrong?" I said. "I just need a minute, Mommy. I'll be okay," she said. I was still upset. "Oh, Nicki, please don't go to class today. We need to go to the clinic and find out what is wrong. I'm worried!" She shook her head. "It's okay, Mommy. This has been happening for a while. I'm going to class. I'll be okay. It goes away."

She didn't want anything keeping her from class, but I just couldn't believe this was happening. Hadn't we been through enough? She doesn't want much—she just wants to go to class. So we sat in the car for about five minutes until she stopped shaking, at which point she got out of the car, gave me a reassuring smile, and said, "Good-bye, Mommy. Don't worry about me, I'll be all right."

I watched her as she very slowly made her way across the parking lot. She'd become so unsteady, and her balance wasn't very good. Fear began creeping into my mind. I prayed, "Please God, please let her get through this class, I'm so scared." I sat in the car with my heart pounding, waiting for two hours until her class would end: I didn't dare leave in case something happened to her. If they had to call an ambulance for some reason, I needed to be there to tell them that she had a brain tumor—if they didn't know, they could do something that might accidentally hurt her. Oh, how I wished she would at least tell her professors!

While sitting there, I called the Nemours Children's Clinic and spoke with her oncologist, Dr. Pitel, and explained to him how she had been shaking. Dr. Pitel could always sense when I was afraid, and he was always there to listen to what Nicki wanted. He knew that Mike wasn't living with us anymore and that I had my hands full, so he did his best to calm me down. Frankly, I had begun to completely rely on him for just about everything now. The only communication between Mike and I now was about Nicki, and he typically didn't come to clinic visits with us because he was working, so it was my responsibility to keep her dad informed about her condition. I knew that Dr. Pitel understood my desperate situation, so I clung to him with all of my being: I was relying on him to save my daughter's life. After all, he was her doctor, the person I counted on to make the right decisions on her behalf. I knew that he was doing everything he could to save my daughter, all while helping me to stay strong and focused on her. How could he deny me? My daughter was dying and my husband had abandoned me. I had no one to turn to, and I had to be strong and healthy for Nicki.

So that day, he was reassuring. "Bring her in right after her class, so we can take another MRI of her brain," he said. I relaxed a little, knowing that he would be waiting to see her whenever we arrived. When I spotted Nicki walking back to the car, I was so relieved; when she got in I gave her a big hug and we drove right away to the clinic. Once there, she underwent another MRI, after which we were told that we would know the results the next day. In spite of this latest episode, I still wanted to believe that the chemo had killed the tumor. Maybe it was denial, but I wasn't going to give up on my hope of a miracle, no matter what. I was no quitter.

Nicki and I were driving home from her class the next day when I got the call from Dr. Pitel. He said that he had the results of her brain scan, and when he asked me to find a place to pull over, I knew that he would be delivering bad news. As Nicki sat next to me, Dr. Pitel told me that the MRI results had revealed her tumor was growing again, and now it was bleeding. "Tumors are very sensitive and often bleed," he said, telling us that this might have caused the shaking episodes that she was experiencing. Again, with this kind of tumor, many things could happen and the cause wasn't always known. But we did know this: a bleeding tumor could cause her death unexpectedly. She could die at any time.

I hung up the phone. I didn't know how I was going to tell Nicki. And yet I could tell she already knew. She was so smart. Who was I kidding? I wasn't kidding myself, and certainly not Nicki. How could she not tell that the report was bad? I knew she could see it on my face, and from the tone of my voice. All I was doing was fooling myself, not her. She knew her body better than anyone; she always seemed to sense when things were changing. And of course, when something was wrong, there were always more tests to be done. Here we were again getting more bad news, I thought. We were trying to survive, but this tumor was out of our control.

As she sat beside me, Nicki had the saddest look on her face. She deserved to know the truth, but for some reason I couldn't tell her. I wasn't sure how to process the news, and wasn't even sure I *wanted* to. I was so removed from reality, living alone in my scary world. I was in complete denial. Why is denial so dangerous? I thought I knew: it's like a powerful drug that seems so comforting, but is totally addictive. It had become my drug, and Nicki knew it. She was trying to help me give it up, but I was too dependent on it. Nicki, though, knew the truth: her sick body had become tired and weak, and she knew the news could only be bad. Yet I still wanted to protect her from the facts because I was afraid she would lose hope. I sometimes wondered if her strength and determination to keep fighting at this point were just for me, as she knew how scared I was of losing her. I wasn't even sure if she really had the strength to keep fighting.

I knew she was nineteen, not a baby any more, and she'd matured so much since fighting cancer. But in my eyes, she was my baby again. I didn't want to see her any other way. Maybe it was time for me to accept that she could die at any time. But I didn't know how to live like that. I wished I could just tell her to lie down and rest. She'd pushed so hard to get well, but now it was beginning to feel as if she was fighting a losing battle. It was so obvious. Still, I wasn't yet ready to give up hope, or come out of denial— a place where I felt comfortable and safe.

EYE OF THE STORM

The 2005 Super Bowl was being held at Alltel Stadium in Jacksonville, and that first week of February the festivities were in full bloom. But our family had nothing to celebrate: Nicki was once again in the hospital. Her doctors said that there wasn't much hope that she would survive at this point, and that she didn't have much time left. I was still reeling from the latest MRI results, having been so positive that the tumor had died. That was supposed to be part of my miracle. Even though I sensed that Nicki had reached acceptance of her future, I had not, and I knew that she worried about me not accepting the fact that she could die at any time now. All I could do was to hold on and never let go, never stop believing that we, that I, would get my miracle.

Nicki was becoming more fragile, and it now became apparent to me that she needed constant medical attention more than ever. In the hospital that day, I looked out the eighth-floor window at the crowded streets below, watching the Super Bowl revelers. My mind wandered to happier times in the past, where I could picture my children sitting in our living room with their dad watching football. Mike would jump for joy when the Jaguars scored. He loved to explain all the plays on the field to the kids, who would ask him a lot of questions, but mostly they were just enjoying being with their dad for that time when he was so happy. He always did love spending time with his children. I wondered if Mike or Jesse were reminiscing like I was. But none of us were talking. We had run out of things to say. We were all in our own world of grief and suffering, silent, as we didn't want Nicki to see or feel our pain. She had enough of her own, and ours would only bring more suffering to her.

While we watched the entire city of Jacksonville on a high that week, the fans so excited to cheer on the Super Bowl teams, it seemed like salt in our wounds. It felt so strange witnessing all of the celebrating outside while we were gathered in a hospital room, knowing that our beloved Nicki could die at any moment. The Super Bowl was the last thing on our minds, but we couldn't make it go away. There was a whole world outside of this hospital room, yet I wondered how I would ever live in it if Nicki died. Would I ever celebrate again? I thought about that possible future every day.

Any time that Nicki was admitted to the hospital, I spent every day and every night with her, sleeping on the rubber cot that was placed in the windowsill. Sometime during this particular weeklong stay, I started losing vision in my right eye. It was as if a curtain was slowly coming down, bringing complete darkness over my sight. I had no idea what could be causing this, but I knew for sure that it couldn't have come at a worse time. Maybe this condition was just psychological—perhaps my body was trying to protect me from seeing what was going on around me. Nicki had recently lost sight in her right eye due to the growing tumor; was my affliction sympathetic? Was my life so entwined with hers that I was now suffering some of her symptoms? Either way, I didn't want her noticing, as I surreptitiously tried to check my vision by covering my left eye. In more ways than one, my world was becoming a dark hole. The eighth floor of the hospital was where young children died: and now it could be my own daughter. How could I even mention my annoying vision problem? I didn't think there was anything I could do about it while Nicki was still in the hospital. What if she died while I was at a doctor's appointment? She came first. *Period.*

Nicki was released a week later, and at the time Dr. Pitel suggested that we have Peds Care, a pediatric health care service for young adult patients, help us at home, but I wouldn't hear of it. I wanted Nicki all to myself. Once she was home safely, I immediately went to the eye doctor, who told me that my retina had detached. No wonder I didn't know what was happening—I had never heard of a retinal detachment and wouldn't have known the symptoms if they hit me in the eye. I was told that I would need surgery immediately or I would go blind in that eye. Mike was no longer living with us, and Jesse had classes to attend, but I just had no choice: I called Mike to tell him that I needed him to take me for surgery the next day. He agreed; next I called my mom and asked her to come up from Fort Myers to stay with Nicki and help us out. And, thank God, she came immediately. The next morning Mike drove me to the hospital and I underwent surgery to have my retina reattached. But though it solved the immediate problem, things became even more difficult for all of us because I was now unable to drive or read for two weeks while I recovered. Nicki had recently lost her ability to read, so we had all been pitching in and taking turns reading to her the past couple of weeks, helping to get her through her classes. Our assistance was very important to her at this time, as she was intent on finishing up the semester, no matter what it took. Now, while I recuperated, my mom was so supportive: she dropped everything in her life to drive up from Fort Myers to help her daughter and granddaughter. The drive from Fort Myers to Jacksonville is seven hours, and if I had let her, my mom would have made it every day.

Thank goodness my surgery was outpatient, so I was able to come home that same day, just wearing a protective eyecup over my eye. I hated to be away from Nicki even for a second, but I needed to go back the next day for a post-op checkup, and then for subsequent follow-up appointments. I ended up wearing the patch over my eye for two weeks as my mom drove me back and forth to my appointments and took Nicki, who was now getting weaker, to her classes. Nicki was on a mission to finish her college classes, no matter what. It was a hectic time, and after all the daily outings when we were finally home, Nicki and I sat together, side by side, on our big La-Z Boy recliner couch while my mom cared for us and read to Nicki every day. With my eye patch and Nicki's limitations, we laughed about the fact that we were now "the blind leading the blind." But the whole time, I was crying inside.

The tumor in Nicki's brain continued to grow every day. I couldn't stop thinking about what could happen. The bleeding could cause her death at any time, so I tried to be thankful for each and every day, every minute and every second that I had with her, even if it was spent inside the four walls of our home. I wanted to keep her with me; I never wanted to let her go. We were together all the time now, and at this point, that's all I cared about. Sitting on our couch, with a patch over my eye, I let my mind wander. I couldn't believe how much our lives had changed and how this stress was affecting our family. It was getting even tougher. I could remember so well when Nicki was a healthy girl, dancing, singing, and reciting lines—page after page—just doing the thing she loved the most, acting. Once upon a time, she was such an incredibly smart and talented girl. Now cancer had taken so much of who she was, though it never destroyed her spirit. She had the most beautiful eyes and they still sparkled, even though behind that sparkle was a brain that wasn't working like it should. She couldn't even remember what her favorite foods were anymore; everything was a struggle. Her doctor kept suggesting that we have Peds Care come to our house to help us, but that was hospice, and I refused to have them here. I didn't want to admit that she was dying—and besides, I wanted her all to myself. I said, flat-out, no. But watching her battle this disease had changed all of our lives. I still wondered why things went so terribly wrong. And I was scared because I didn't know how I would ever survive if I lost Nicki.

My mom did what most moms do: she came to help us in our time of need. With this latest hurdle to jump, we wanted her here with us. She was the best, always willing to do whatever she could to take care of her family. Nicki loved her—especially loved her cheesy mashed potatoes, which Grandma made several times for her while she was there. I could never make them like my mom did, and Nicki knew it! My mom ran errands and picked up medications, as well as cleaned the house and cooked our meals, but it was her mothering love that I really needed at this time, and she gave it to both of us so beautifully. We were three generations of women in the house, going through a great deal of pain together and leaning on one another for strength, love, and compassion. The precious time Nicki got to spend with her grandmother was important to both of them. I loved how my mom would take over soothing

Nicki for a while so that I could rest, and my daughter didn't have to worry about me as much. And when her grandma wasn't around, Nicki would always ask when she was coming. She knew that if things ever got too bad—which happened on several occasions—Grandma would be the first one to show up to help us and love us. Without my mom, I don't know how we would have managed during this time.

She would have stayed with us forever, but I wanted our life to remain as normal as possible, so once I could drive again, I sent her home. I hoped that Nicki and I could manage with some help from Jesse now, as I knew he would do whatever he could. Keeping my mom around would have been good for Nicki, and I know that now, but I was hoarding my daughter. I wanted her all to myself.

Not surprisingly, Nicki managed to keep up with her classes despite her problems. She was more determined than ever, and even though school was starting to get a lot harder for her, she continued to give it all that she had, and then some. I tried to persuade her to tell her professors about her cancer, but she wouldn't hear of it, and I respected her choice. It made me so sad to see her struggle at school, though; she was once so bright, but now, with her handicaps, learning was a challenge as things began to change rapidly—and not for the better.

One day, as I was driving her to school, Nicki said something that didn't make sense, a phrase like, "The red truck at the dog." As soon as she said it she realized what had just come out of her mouth, but didn't understand how or why. We looked at each other questioningly. With a worried look on her face, she asked, "Mommy, what did I just say?" I told her that I wasn't sure, but I thought that we should turn around and go home. It scared both of us that, apparently, the thought she'd had in her mind hadn't translated into a meaningful sentence. This was a new and frightening development in her condition.

As time went on, this disturbing condition progressed to the point that Nicki couldn't put words together at all. She would get so frustrated when she wanted to say something and couldn't, so she just didn't talk much anymore. I pleaded with her to keep trying to communicate with me, and I assured her that I could understand her, but it became hard for her to get her point across. Continuing to try to talk became a huge challenge for her, and it took a lot of her energy, all of which caused *more* stress, something we were always trying to alleviate. After seeing her neuro-oncologist at the Mayo Clinic in Jacksonville, the doctor thought that this condition might reverse itself and that her speech would come back to normal, but in the end it didn't. I appreciated that he was always full of hope just like me, but medicine was failing us. Now, I relied even more on a miracle. With each passing day, I watched Nicki grow weaker, and more and more uncontrollable changes kept happening to her. One day, while we were standing in the kitchen, she poured a glass of water and, as she held it in her hand, it seemed to just fall to the floor where it shattered. We were both startled, but knew that it wasn't a simple accident: she had lost feeling in her arm. Now she couldn't hold anything that could break.

On April 5, 2005, Nicki was intent on taking me out for dinner to celebrate my birthday, so we went to one of our favorite restaurants, Ruby Tuesday. Nicki loved their salad bar, especially their German potato salad. Looking back, I think that she wanted to make sure she was able to celebrate my birthday with me in case it was the last one we would share together as mother and daughter. Knowing Nicki, she would want me to have a special memory to last a lifetime. I wasn't thinking at all that way, because I still wouldn't let my mind go there. I was still trying to act like everything was fine, even though it was so evident that it wasn't.

After finishing our meal, she insisted on paying the bill; it was her treat: she was trying to take care of me. She knew her time was running out. I could see the signs that things were continuing to go downhill. As I watched her take the pen in her hand, I became aware of how difficult it was for her to sign our check; her small, delicate hands were now so unsteady, still dainty and beautiful despite the fact that they were cracked, raw and red from all the hand washing she had to do avoid an immune system–compromising infection. Looking at her fingers, I thought how lovely they were, and that her perfectly manicured nails showed me her elegance and grace, qualities that cancer could not steal from her. She still had dimples on her knuckles. We always used to tease her about that, and I smiled to remember that. These were tangible things, details that I hadn't observed closely for a while now.

As she pushed the pen across the paper and scribbled her signature, my eyes began to water. Her determination to push through what was clearly a losing battle against time was so obvious. I watched her desperately grip the pen to sign our check. She had become weaker every day, and the effects from the steroids that caused her body to swell— yet tragically did *not* un-swell her brain—had worn on her. It sure had taken a toll on my baby. She was so fragile and soft; she would forever be my sweet baby girl. I found it so ironic that her signature now looked like a young child's. But I couldn't go any further with that kind of thinking because she *had* to recover. I knew it was my responsibility to help her put her affairs in order, if that was what she wanted, but I just couldn't—not yet. Why couldn't I do this for her? Why couldn't I accept that she was simply too tired to keep going? She needed me to be strong for her, but I knew I was never going to be able to let go of her, and she knew that I couldn't. I needed her in my life. I wouldn't imagine it without her.

One morning, as I stepped out of the shower, Nicki walked into my room already dressed for the day in her signature blue jeans and white tank top. She sat with her head against the headboard and her legs stretched out over my bed. As I stood there with a towel wrapped around my body and another around my head, she looked over and said, "Mommy, it's hard." I quivered inside. I knew she was trying to tell me that my miracle might not happen, and that I needed to prepare myself to face losing her, but I couldn't—or wouldn't—see it then. At this point, there were times when she could talk and times when she couldn't. It was sporadic, and although we had learned how to communicate with gestures and very basic sign language, I treasured her words when she could talk. I thought about how much I loved that she still called me "Mommy," even at nineteen years old, and I knew that I would miss it so much. Sons just don't do that and, well, my son never had.

But these words pierced my soul, and my heart sank when she said that, having never said anything like that before. She was always so positive, and though she had always known how hard her cancer was for all of *us*, she never admitted that it was hard for *her*. I knew it was coming, though: the fear that she was not winning her war against cancer. It ripped at my heartstrings. Her frail body was getting more and more unsteady, and her vision loss and balance problems made it hard for her to get around on her own. She couldn't remember things or communicate with us very well, and she was painfully aware of this. It was frustrating, and stressful, and required a lot of her energy. She kept dropping things often and was quickly becoming less independent. This was not how she wanted to live. I knew that she wanted to talk to me about letting go, but I couldn't have that conversation. *Just keep fighting*, I thought, yet at the same time I knew that Nicki had already accepted that she wasn't going to live very much longer. Now, as she tried to begin the process of putting her affairs in order, she wanted my permission to let go.

During this time, I worried a lot about Jesse too. These were supposed to be the best years of his young adult life, and I was heartbroken that he was being forced to live with so much uncertainty and pain—both from watching his sister dying from cancer, and from watching his parents' marriage dissolve. My husband and I had completely stopped communicating with each other, and I was reserving all my energy for Nicki. After Mike had moved out, I leaned on Jesse as a stabilizing force for Nicki and me, looking to him to help us, which he gladly did. We both needed a man around, and he was always there to help us, stepping up to the plate and becoming our main source of strength. We knew that we could always rely on Jesse, and that he wanted to be close to Nicki. He cared about his sister so much and would do anything for her. As siblings he and Nicki had always been close, only twenty-three months apart in age; they had even elected to go to the same high school. Nicki always looked up to Jesse, and for his part he had always treated her with respect and protection. They certainly had shared a lot of laughter together through the years. They always leaned on each other for everything, and now Nicki was leaning on her brother in a much different way, one that had never before seemed imaginable or real—but it was real. And it was painful.

As Nicki continued to lose strength, I knew it was going to be hard for her to finish out the last week of school and to take her final exams. I tried to talk her into just leaving school, telling her that it didn't matter, but it mattered to *her*, and she was going to finish her freshman year of college no matter what; nothing was going to stop her. She knew, though, that she didn't have the strength to do it on her own, so she asked Jesse and I if we would accompany her to school. This was the only time she had ever asked anyone for help. We knew how important it was for her to complete the school year, as it was part of her mission to put her affairs in order. I didn't realize it at the time; I just wanted her home, safe, all to myself. I was afraid that it would be too much for her, and wanted her to just stay home so I could watch her every minute of the day. But finally I realized that she really hadn't changed: my fearless daughter was not a quitter, and now she wanted to finish this semester. It was going to be extremely hard for me to let her do it—and it would be extremely hard for her to do on her own—but Jesse and I knew that, with or without our acceptance, she would follow her heart, as she had always done before. So, we assured her that we would help.

Since Jesse was also attending UNF, we decided it was time that he talked to Nicki's professors to let them know that Nicki had a brain tumor and was nearing the end of her life, as now, suddenly, it was very important that they know. There were two professors that Nicki had grown especially fond of: her English professor, Dr. Menocal, and her math professor, Dr. Joe Flowers. So Jesse called and made appointments to meet with both of them individually. It was especially hard for Jesse to tell these two professors about Nicki because they had played such a big role in her college life, and when Jesse delivered the news, they both were shocked and saddened. They had both seen signs of her struggle, but never suspected anything like *this*. Jesse explained why she hadn't told them at the beginning of the semester, letting them know how she had just wanted to blend in and didn't want any special attention given to her. But they both agreed that Nicki was too special to ever just blend in. Dr. Menocal told Jesse he had noticed that Nicki looked tired sometimes and had been concerned about her, but that she was always such a joy to have in his class, always working hard, and with a smile; Dr. Menocal offered to assist her any way that he could, as did Dr. Flowers, her math professor. He, like Dr. Menocal, was deeply saddened when Jesse delivered the news to him. He said that Nicki had been doing so well, and that she was the "brightest student in his class." Jesse let them know how important it was for Nicki to take her final exams, and they understood and agreed to let Jesse assist her in any way he wished.

Now that Jesse had talked to her professors, we made a plan to accompany Nicki to UNF and help her with her final classes so that she would be able to take her exams and finish out the semester. The school arranged for Nicki to use a private room where Jesse could assist her by reading the exam questions to her, since she couldn't read anymore. During the exam, Jesse would read a question to Nicki; he would then give her the multiple-choice answers, such as A, B, C, or D. Due to her confusion and difficulty communicating, Nicki would often answer "F" or "Q." It was extremely hard for Jesse to watch his sister in this state of mind, but he would just circle the answer he knew was right and continue on.

After completing her exams, Nicki wanted to go to the school cafeteria and treat Jesse to pizza for lunch, because they had often met there for lunch together, and she knew how much he loved pizza. Since she was so weak, I wanted to drive the three of us to the other side of the campus, but she was intent on walking across her college campus one last time: she wanted to take this walk with her brother, and asked Jesse to help because she couldn't walk by herself. I headed toward the car, as I was going to drive to the other side of the campus to meet them, since I knew it would be too much for her to walk back. For a moment, I turned back to look at them and memorize the image of my two children—my son, so strong and healthy, and my daughter, so weak and sick. Seeing that, I was consumed by tears. I will never forget that image as long as I live, nor will I forget the desperation I felt when I saw Nicki lean her unsteady body on her brother's strong shoulder. He put his arm around her waist and pulled her close to him as they proceeded to walk, ever so slowly, across campus together. I was unaware of anyone around me; I couldn't turn away. I just watched my children as they held onto each other, maybe for the last time ever.

While walking and holding onto her brother for support, Nicki spoke haltingly, thanking Jesse for nineteen years of love, saying her own special good-bye to the brother who protected her all her life—the brother she would be leaving behind—the brother she loved with her whole heart. Watching my two children walking together that day will always be one of the strongest memories that I hold in my heart.

I knew, at that moment, that my daughter was still clinging to life by a thread of hope— a thread that was weakening before my eyes. When we got home, Nicki asked me if we could go on the computer to sign her up for summer classes. Just in case.

FINAL RIDE

On April 26, I woke every hour so that I could check on Nicki, as had become my normal habit. It was three am, and I noticed a light coming from Nicki's room down the hall, which was unusual. Concerned, I followed the light down the hall and, finding her door open, I entered. I had walked this path many times in the past fifteen years, but it was different now. Before cancer, I had usually heard laughter coming from her room; since cancer, mostly I heard vomiting. Fortunately, she was quiet tonight. I looked in and was surprised to see her sitting up in her bed with her television on. Great, I thought, this seems okay. But I really knew that it wasn't. She had a strange look on her face: her eyes didn't look the same; she was staring straight ahead, but it seemed that she wasn't focused on anything. She didn't seem to be in pain or look distressed, but I knew that something wasn't right. Since I didn't know what to do, I said, "You can't sleep either?" Her hands gestured for me to go back to bed, so I did. It bothered her how I was always checking on her, as if I was consumed with caring for her and could never relax—which was true.

Back in my room, as I lay in bed, my mind raced with all kinds of thoughts that I just couldn't get a hold of. Should I have let Peds Care help us? But I just couldn't have let strangers interfere with my daughter's final days. I had taken care of her this long; I didn't want them here. Was I wrong, though? I had watched her grow weaker in the last month, and her breathing had become labored, but no, I still wouldn't accept that she was going to die.

I prayed: Please, God, can I just walk in her room one

morning and find her quiet and peaceful, like Sleeping Beauty? Then she will be free from pain and suffering, and there won't be any painful good-byes. But, she would want to say good-bye, and I couldn't deny her that. I just didn't want to say it too soon. I couldn't let her go. There had been so much pain for all of us the past three years—watching her have seizures, vomiting, and taking all those pills that weren't even working. We ere all exhausted, and the worst thing for her was that she knew it. We didn't want her to know how it was killing us, and yet she told me that she knew it was harder for us than for her. Now it was time for me to be strong. I didn't want her to worry about us, but she did anyway.

Painful situations never seem to go the way we imagine them to or go the way we want them to, I thought. No one was in control of this situation except God, and at this point it didn't appear that He was going to grant my miracle. As I lay there, I began to sob. My bed should have been a waterbed by then, from the million tears of desperation that I had cried alone the last three years. Deep down, there had always been a glimmer of hope that I still carried inside of me, hoping that she would go back to sleep, wake up, and be fine the next morning.

Without realizing how much time had passed, I suddenly heard Nicki vomiting. This was never a good sign, because it meant her brain was swelling again. I realized that it was now six o'clock as I rushed into her room. As soon as I saw her, I immediately called her doctors. "Help me, please!" I cried to the switchboard operator, but the doctor wasn't in yet. I went back to Nicki, knelt beside her bed, and asked her if she was in pain. She couldn't answer me—she couldn't talk.

When the clinic finally reached her doctor, he immediately called me back and advised me to increase her steroids so the pressure in her brain would go down, but she couldn't swallow the pills. Sobbing, I called Mike. "Hurry! Nicki's dying, and we have to get her to the hospital!" I cried. When I hung up the phone, I was in shock. I was so afraid that this was it. Peds Care would have come days ago, but I had been in denial. I should have listened to her doctor when he told me she could die any day and that Peds Care could help me. But I had been trusting God to heal her. Oh please, God. Somebody help me!

When Mike arrived, he came running into the house and found us in Nicki's room, where she was lying on her bed as I dressed her in sweat pants and a T-shirt. Mike picked her up in his arms and carried her limp body out to my car, laying her in the back seat. Jesse went to comfort his little sister, and as he did I could see the pain in his face. We put a pillow under her head and wrapped her in a blanket, trying to help her to be more comfortable, but we could see her discomfort; I thought that, for the first time in three years, she looked truly afraid. Her eyes looked different—they had lost the twinkle. She stared at us in such a desperate way, as if to say, "Help me, please!" That's when I knew that we couldn't drive her ourselves, so I grabbed the phone and dialed 911. It was Nicki's third and final ride in an ambulance to Wolfson Children's Hospital. I knew she wouldn't want it to happen this way; if this was her time to go, she wouldn't want it to be there. She *hated* being in the hospital—but they always fixed her and she had always come home, and that's what I was hoping for again.

Nicki had already endured so much pain and suffering,

and usually felt relieved when the ambulance arrived to take her to help, but this time was different. When it pulled up in front of our house, she became more afraid, not comforted by its presence. Five young men, not that much older than Nicki, stepped out of the ambulance. Why were there so many men here, I wondered? I thought it must have been humiliating for Nicki with those good-looking young men surrounding her as she lay on a stretcher in so much pain, unable to even talk. When I told them that her doctor was waiting for her at Wolfson's Children's Hospital, they said that they couldn't transport her there because it was out of their county. *What?*—I panicked!

"You have to take her there," I said. "Her doctor is meeting us there!" Immediately, I called Dr. Pitel, crying; he told me to let him talk to the paramedics, and when I handed the driver my cell phone, he was able to clear up all of the confusion. Next, the paramedics moved Nicki from the back of my car onto a stretcher, then placed her in the back of the ambulance. I rode in the front next to the driver, while Mike and Jesse followed us. All the way to the hospital, there was total silence from the back, where Nicki was lying on a stretcher surrounded by these young paramedics. But the silence couldn't stop the screaming that was going on in my head as I talked non-stop to the driver. What did I say? I have no idea, although I remember what I was thinking: What was going on? Was this the end? It couldn't be. This was my baby. My baby can't die! Why was I sitting up here in the front with the driver when I should be in the back with Nicki, holding her? She needed to know I was there and that I loved her with my whole heart. Don't die, Nicki. Mommy's right here.

Nothing seemed real to me in any way; it was as if my

mind wasn't functioning in the present anymore, and I couldn't comprehend time or handle what was taking place. I was trying to act normal, but I didn't know what normal was anymore. The ambulance driver must have thought I was crazy—but what did I care what he thought anyway? My baby was dying! Who were these strangers? I thought we were all supposed to die with family around us, at home in our own bed. It was my fault that it wasn't happening that way for Nicki.

Finally, at the hospital, I calmed down a little and felt better because her doctors were there. They always helped her here, and she always came home. I held her hand as two young men wheeled her on the stretcher into the hospital, then brought her to a small, gloomy ER with various gadgets all over the place. Then, they left us alone. It was so cold in there. As I stood beside her still, frail body, I was stunned and quiet. Her eyes were closed, and she looked relaxed and peaceful, so I didn't want to disturb her after all the trauma she just went through. I wondered what she was thinking, but I didn't say anything. I was just so scared, tired, and numb.

I slowly moved closer to her and just kept staring at her beautiful young face, but I was still afraid to touch her. Though I was scared, I felt content to be alone with her now because she seemed so peaceful. Tomorrow she was supposed to start a new chemo treatment, ordered by her doctor at the Mayo Clinic. He had so much hope that she would survive. He's like me, I thought, because we were both so sure that she could beat this thing, and that *this* time the new chemo would kill the tumor. Please, God, one more day; please don't let this be the end.

Nicki lay there, more beautiful than Sleeping Beauty—

but this was real, not a fairy tale. She hadn't opened her eyes or moved at all. I continued to study her angelic face, looking down at her, praying, but also relieved that she didn't seem to be in pain. Then, without moving the rest of her body or opening her eyes, Nicki reached out to me. Instantly I felt this sense of desperation come from her, something that she had never shown before. I lovingly took her hand in mine as she squeezed my hand tightly. Where was her strength coming from? I wondered. She was grasping for me, clinging to me, and I to her. At this moment we didn't want to let go of each other. We held on, clutching each other's hand; my body felt warm, and I became very calm. This was the moment that I had never wanted to come, the one I had avoided for so long. But now, I knew that Nicki wanted my permission to go. How was I going to let her go? I couldn't let her go. But now I had to. I had to do something, so I spoke beyond reality and into eternity.

Staying calm, I squeezed her hand gently; she kept a firm hold of my hand, not wanting to let go of me. I had held that hand for nineteen years. I knew it so well. I could remember the first time she wrapped her tiny hand around my finger. How could I ever let go, when I still wanted to hold on and never let go? How many times did I hold this hand to protect her while crossing the street or in a crowd? But now our situation was reversed. I was holding her hand in order to let her go. Not wanting to lose our embrace, my touch assured her that I loved her with all of my being. I couldn't begin to count the kisses that had been blown to me with this tender loving hand. Now it was saying to me, "Mommy, I don't want to leave you, but I must."

I didn't embrace her. I don't know why. In a whispered

voice, I said to her, "It's over, Nicki." She immediately released my hand, but then quickly reached out to me again. That's not what she wanted to hear from me, because she knew that now her pain and suffering would be over. Carefully, I took her hand again and then said, "Go into the arms of Jesus, now." And, once again, she let go of my hand; but now she quickly reached out to me a third time, squeezing my hand even tighter now. I could tell she was desperate for me to say good-bye. I bent down closer to her face, and I softly spoke. "Mommy will be all right."

With these words, she let go of my hand and drifted off into a coma. She looked satisfied, and I felt relief for the first time in three years, because now I knew that she would also be all right. She had waited long enough to hear these words from me, the very words that I had never been able to say to her before now. But this time, I knew that I needed to set her free. And I also knew I would always and forever keep my promise to my daughter, no matter what life would bring to me: I knew I would never be great again, but I would honor her wish, and I would always make sure that I was at least "all right."

I could now thank God for granting me my miracle. Although not the way I wanted it to happen, He finally answered my prayers: Nicki was pain-free and, now, set free at last. This metaphorical experience that I had shared with my daughter was a gift, and I knew it. I dropped my head and heard her voice. "Thank you, Mommy."

I wasn't aware of how much time had passed before Dr. Pitel came rushing into the room. He was in a panic, but this time I was finally at peace. While he examined Nicki, I stood back, looking at her lying there. She truly looked peaceful and pain-free. Dr. Pitel and I had spent so many desperate times like this together with her; I thought of all the times I called him because I was afraid and didn't know what to do. He was always there with instructions that calmed me down. Would this be the end of our relationship with my daughter? He so had wanted her to live. At this time I realized how much I relied on him. He was so good to Nicki, always putting her needs and feeling first, but he was also there for me when I needed him.

I watched him as he carefully looked Nicki over, then confirmed that she was in a coma. We both just stood there, looking at each other with sadness. He had been her doctor for almost three years, trying to save her life. But it still wasn't completely over: Nicki was still alive—not conscious, but alive. Now she was once again transported to the eighth floor, Oncology, where we met up with Mike and Jesse. And it was there that she would lie for three days before taking her last breath. The hospital staff knew that she was going to die, so they gave her a room closest to the nursing station, where we were treated like royalty, and Nicki the queen. We couldn't have been anyplace safer than where we were right then; it almost felt like our home away from home by now.

During this time, my mother came and sat with Nicki, talking to her and never leaving her side. My mom must have been so sad sitting next to her bed every day, never leaving. I knew she was there talking to Nicki, touching her, loving her. At this point, my grief had consumed me beyond belief. Everything was foggy; I was exhausted, somewhat in shock, but yet I was also relieved. I had had three years to say all that I wanted to, so now I felt relief to see her finally at peace. Along with my mom, some of Jesse's close friends came to see Nicki and to support Jesse during this time, as well as other family members and friends. They all came to say good-bye to her and to show their love for our family.

Over the next three days, I felt a deep parting, and yet an incredible release. Although I waited until the last minute, I finally came to a place of acceptance, and I was thankful that God provided that private time where I could finally let her go and promise Nicki that I would be all right. Around 11:30 pm on the third night, when all the visitors had left, Mike, Jesse, and I were preparing our beds, exhausted after a long day. Mike sat in a large fabric chair, while Jesse went to lay on a wide ledge with a cushion by the window. I curled up on the only leather reclining chair in her room. I had positioned myself beside Nicki's bed so that I would be lying directly beside her. I leaned my mouth close to her ear and whispered, "Good night, my sweet baby," then kissed her cheek.

Resting my head close to hers, I could hear and feel her breathing. I wanted to be sure that I would be touching her when she took her last breath. About an hour into the night, as her breathing became more shallow, I drew closer to her body. She took a deep breath in, and somehow we all knew this one was her last. All three of us gathered tightly around our beautiful girl; we knew this was our last good-bye. Jesse placed his hand over his little sister's heart and kept it there until her heart stopped beating. We all bowed our heads in sorrow. It was final. Then, I lifted my head, and I felt heaven's gates open as Nicki went into the arms of Jesus.

Nineteen years before, God had given us the most wonderful gift, a baby girl. We named her Nicki. He couldn't have given me anything as precious or dear to my heart as she was to me then, and always will be. I know that I will miss her every day for the rest of my life.

AFTER THE STORM

I cut a lock of Nicki's silky blonde hair and put it in a small white satin-lined box for safekeeping. Then I gently and lovingly bathed her, while she lay on the hospital bed, then dressed her in soft white cotton pajamas, provided by the hospital. When I had finished, Mike and Jesse came into the room, and we gathered once again around her. Together, we told Nicki that we loved her; we all kissed her goodbye. Then I assured my daughter again that although I would never be *great* without her, I would be "all right," as I had promised her in the end. When two men, hospital employees, came to take her away, I hugged them both and asked them to be extra-gentle with her. After all, she was my baby.

We held Nicki's funeral at the church where she had grown up singing and performing. Pastor Cooper officiated through tears to a church filled with Nicki's family, friends, and even well-wishers who never knew her. Our family wore all black in mourning: this was not a celebration, rather a tearful goodbye to a remarkable young woman who had suffered for three years and yet never stopped smiling. We knew that one day we would see her again, but right now we needed to grieve. Pastor Cooper had been Jesse and Nicki's youth pastor, and it was comforting to have him perform her going-away service here in this church. The funeral was the day before Mother's Day. I remember the church lighting was dim and the atmosphere was mournful, but also calm and peaceful. Many of the mourners wiped tears from their eyes while watching videos of Nicki standing on this stage, performing with so much emotion. We never expected or imagined that one day we would be watching her performances while attending her funeral.

One of the videos showed a fourteen-year-old Nicki portraying Mary, Mother of God, during a Christmas Eve service. I smile to remember how excited Nicki was when she came home from the auditions and Priscilla, Nicki's voice teacher, had called and told me that she had chosen Nicki for the role of Mary because of her elegance and grace at such a young age. Nicki had been so happy to be chosen because, while singing, she would get to hold a real baby in her arms. Another video showed her singing the song "Lamb of God" in her sweet soprano voice, when she was just sixteen. A third video was a gift from DASOTA, carefully put together by Lorry Romano, a gifted teacher from the video and film department. Many of Nicki's school friends had stayed up all night helping Lorry put together this memorial video for the funeral; it was a photo essay of Nicki through the years: pictures of her with family and friends, singing, dancing, and acting—all the passions that she had while here on this earth.

While Mike, Jesse, and I sat in the front row of the pews watching the video from DASOTA, I thought about what Dr. Beger had said about Nicki when she heard the sad news of her passing. She said that Nicki "truly sparkled on stage, and had amazing abilities as a singer, dancer, and actress." But what touched me the most was when Dr. Beger told me how Nicki's classmates loved her and looked to her for guidance. "After Nicki became ill," she told me, "one after another of her friends came to me, asking how they could help her because she had given so much to them. We lost a star—not only on stage, but more importantly, a star that, through her generosity of spirit, guided us all."

Nicki's friend Ryan gave an unforgettable eulogy for his "Nick Nick," calling her a gifted performer with quiet beauty and elegance. He told us how hard it was for him to be so far from her while she battled cancer, and remembered their many hours-long phone calls. He had a beautiful line in particular: "Her long-distance laughter could melt my heart." Then he said, "I loved Nicki from the bottom of my heart. I don't think I will ever feel that way about anyone again." Finally, reaching into his pocket, Ryan pulled out a note from Nicki, which he told us imparted a very profound message that, he said, "means even more to me today." Nicki had written: "Don't frown because it's over... Smile because it happened." After reading her quote to the audience, Ryan added, "I'm smiling, Nick Nick. I love you."

I believe that Nicki was smiling from heaven as she heard Ryan repeat those words. We all bowed our heads, tears in our eyes. After the funeral, we had a sunset burial at St. Justin the Martyr Orthodox Church, where she would be the first burial at the new cemetery. Before she was buried, Mike, Jesse, and I each gave Nicki one last kiss. I looked at my daughter one last time, as she lay holding the icon of Jesus that I had placed in her hand at her private viewing. Then, we said good-bye. Nicki passed away on April 29, shortly after my birthday and just one day before my mother turned seventy. After her death, I was numb for weeks, just going through the motions of daily life. I tried to remember my promise to Nicki that I would be all right, but did I have to start so *soon* after losing her? Couldn't I just have some time to grieve first, Nicki?

I found that writing helped a great deal, and since I had

always had a passion for writing—and now that I suddenly had more time than I knew what to do with—I started a new journal. It not only gave me a way to pour out my emotions, but also allowed me to capture all of our memories. The following is a typical entry from that first month:

My mind often travels mysteriously to another place where there is no sickness and no death, where streets are paved in gold and there is no more pain or suffering. I am going to spend eternity in this place, the only place where I am promised to hold my child once again—my baby girl who developed in my womb, suckled at my breast, and accompanied me as my daughter, friend, and mentor for nineteen years. My Nicki, she died too soon. I should, but I can't touch my sadness. I want to embrace the sorrow and feel the pain. I can't stop the flow at times like this when I think about the tumor in her brain that took her from me. My face was once young and vibrant, but is now aged with sorrow. The tumor took almost everything, her witty sense of humor and so many of her memories, but it could not take her spirit, and it never stole her charm.

She knew me deeply to the end, probably more powerfully than at any other time during her nineteen years. I know that I am blessed to have known a love as extraordinary as we shared the last years of her life. She was my teacher, my mentor, and I admired her. Cancer brought emotion wrought with passion to her being.

As time has passed, I've filled my journal with entries like these, as I try to process my grief and confront the reality of what happened.

These are things you lose, that you can't get back, only memories of the times that are now written on the pages of diaries and memoirs.

I closed my journal, and put my pencil down.

The last three years have taken a toll on my body, but now it's Nicki's spirit that keeps me vibrant and focused. My son Jesse is a healing balm for my broken heart, reminding me that he is alive, breathing, and that we are also connected. This, for me, is life after death.

Now, when teardrops slide down my cheek and into my mouth, I just swallow the salty sadness and hear Nicki say to me, "Be happy, Mommy." I have to be, for I know this pain: it's called grief, and it comes in waves, like the ocean, washing over me a little harder at this time of year, spring. Spring: my favorite season, when the air smells sweet and Nicki's favorite white oleander tree starts to bloom. On our walks to the beach, we used to pass by it hundreds of times. Now, its poisonous petals remind me that something so beautiful can also grow something so deadly.

Which, I think, is kind of like the visits to my mailbox lately, where I now receive two types of mail: pastel envelopes full of kind words and shared memories of Nicki, sent from loved ones and friends; and plain white business envelopes—those are the ones from divorce attorneys.

REMORSE

Jesse was now the only one I had left from our original family of four, and I thanked God for him every day. My son continued to bless my life in so many ways, and I felt that now, finally, I could concentrate on him for a while, especially since, now that I was alone, I wasn't sure what I was going to do with my life. Jesse and I had always been close and, up until the time Nicki became sick, I had spent a lot of time with him. When your child attends a school for the performing arts, even normal life is incredibly busy: there were visits to colleges, auditions, performances, award ceremonies, receptions where Jesse played guitar, and graduation parties. But when Nicki's symptoms started appearing at the end of Jesse's senior year of high school, I began to miss huge parts of his life, and I now realized just how much had gone by without me. All of my time had been devoted to her, leaving Jesse to pretty much fend for himself—when he wasn't helping us, that is. Fortunately, Jesse had wanted to spend all the time he could with his sister, helping her with schoolwork and including her in everything he did—even taking her along when he went out with friends.

After Nicki's death, Jesse and I changed roles: I was now a single parent, and he was an only child. I tried to understand how difficult things had been for him. Losing his sister was enough to contend with, but then watching his parents' twenty-three-year marriage crumble during this same time... well, that was more than any teenager should have to bear. It seemed as though he had lost almost everything that was stable in his life, and yet he managed to have a stabilizing effect on all of us, as he had his whole life. As much as I wanted to continue to depend on Jesse after Nicki passed away, I knew that I needed to let him go back to living his life. He would always be there for me if I needed him, but now he wanted his independence, and I knew he deserved it. And, seeing Jesse move forward with his life gave me so much strength and joy; I hoped he would find a way to leave behind his pain so he could start fresh. Jesse was confident that I would be all right, and I thought so too, even though I wasn't sure what I was going to do immediately. But I did know, at least, that I had to figure it out alone. This was a time for me to be still.

After thinking more about it, I realized that my family of four had, in fact, dwindled down to just me. Jesse, as I had hoped, was living his own life, and I wasn't sure what my destiny held. Gradually, I learned to enjoy the solitude and the quiet. I very seldom watched TV or played music; those things just reminded me of the past and brought back too many sad memories. Every time I turned on the TV, it seemed like episodes of "I Love Lucy" and "Let's Make a Deal," two of Nicki's favorite shows, were on; the radio still played songs that Nicki and I listened to while driving back and forth to her treatments. I didn't want sad reminders of the past: I was trying to move forward and be better than "all right." I wanted to be *happy.* I treasured the sound of the waves on the shore, the birds chirping, and even learned to enjoy the quiet of nothing but my own thoughts.

Besides seeing some of my very close friends, I chose to embrace my solitude. I found it difficult to be out in the world, and although people meant well, most of them really didn't sccm comfortable around me. "I can't even imagine what it's like to lose a child," they would tell me. But I thought that if they would allow themselves to imagine my pain—or anyone else's pain who had lost a child—they would be able to just fine. They just didn't *want* to go there, so it created a wall that divided us. It made me feel isolated: just like young adults feel when they get cancer, I imagined, which helped me to understand even more how Nicki felt. It hurt to the core to be different. I felt like most people who knew me were thinking, "Glad I'm not walking in her shoes."

But I had never thought this would happen to me, either. Never. But it did, and there was no escaping reality. It happened. I had accepted this fate and I now was dealing with what God had chosen and planned for my life. I wanted to experience real, loving relationships with people again, but I couldn't, unless they were willing to enter my pain. The fear of losing a child is every parent's worst nightmare. Think about it: don't know how you would ever survive the pain? Let me tell you, the truth is, you would if you *had* to—just like we all did. Just so you know, it's just what you imagine: horrific, painful, tormenting, and sad. The best way I could ever describe it is that it's your worst nightmare come to life, and then you have no place to hide your fear and misery because now you're an open book for everyone to see. It's such a personal thing, and yet you're thrown into public display while you are grieving. I want to tell people, "I'm just like you. I just have another side of being a parent that you may not."

Now, at least, Nicki is never a source of concern for me. Yes, she suffered, but I'm peaceful knowing that she is with God. Jesse is here with me and, like every parent, I still worry about him at times. But it's not comforting when people tell me, "At least you still have another child," or "At least Nicki's in a better place." And then there are comments like, "I know how you feel. My grandma died this year." My grandparents died, as well as my dad, but it doesn't compare to losing a child.

That summer, I spent my time trying to focus on the positive—that Nicki was no longer in pain and that she was finally at peace. And, I'd had nineteen unforgettable years with her. I had promised her that I would be happy, but I wasn't there yet. I was still too raw and, with the new quiet in my life, I could see more clearly and found that I had some regrets. I spent a great deal of time thinking and praying, curled up on the sofa, writing in my journal. I knew I had to work my way through some regrets before I could begin to move forward.

So, I wrote my heart out. As I did, I remembered when Nicki was so confused, when she knew something was wrong but nobody understood her. That was when she started taking long walks on the beach to sort things out. As I considered Nicki's walks, I wondered if I might have been able to save my marriage with such meditation and reflection myself, but I had been so wrapped up in my pain and grief, consumed with how I would survive when Nicki died.

I stopped writing and closed my journal. Then, heading for the door, I laced up my sneakers and stepped outside. It was a hot August day, and it didn't take long before I was drenched in sweat from the heat and humidity. When I got to the beach, it was covered with a thick layer of fog. My eyes seemed blurry from the overwhelming mist; I couldn't make out anything, because the sea and sky appeared to have become one: moisture from the clouds and steam from the ocean, combined with heat from the sun, had caused a thick haze over everything. Everything was foggy, just like my mind. But I had come to figure things out: while I felt that I had done many things right, I knew I had also made mistakes, thinking that I was doing the right thing at the time. As I walked along the shore, the sun pierced the clouds, and its warmth slowly began to melt the fog. As the day cleared, my mind began to settle. While the mighty surf crashed against the shore, the sun burned through the fog; I could now begin to see the blue sky above, and my thoughts continued to clear. The things I had done right, as well as the mistakes I had made: they were both a part of me. I could sort it out, right here, today, on this beach.

There had been so many things that Nicki wanted to do, and so many people with whom she'd wanted to make memories, including her best friends Katie and Ryan, but cancer had held her hostage in Jacksonville. It made me think now about why it's so important not to wait to do the things you love and spend time with people you love. I wanted to tell everybody, "Go see your best friends and show them how much they mean to you. Get busy building memories!" I had kept telling Nicki that when she got better, she could go visit Ryan and Katie, who were both studying acting, the same thing that Nicki loved, but I knew I couldn't let her go. I was too afraid to let her fly because she was so sick. It must have been terrible for her to see her best friends living their dream while she was living a nightmare. And in the end, she never got better: her time ran out, and it was too late.

I wish now that I had called Katie and Ryan to let them know how sick she had become. I should have asked for them to come to her—they would have, no questions asked—but at the end I wanted Nicki all to myself. I didn't want to share her. After Nicki died, Katie told me that Nicki had seemed so happy that last week they spent together, and how they'd had so much fun. Katie said, "I truly thought that Nicki was going to be okay." I remember that week as one of Nicki's happiest times. I know I should have called Katie and told her how sick Nicki really was. I'm sorry for that.

I thought about Nicki and Matt. When we took Nicki to Tampa to visit him, that was the last time she would see him in person. Although they continued to talk, as Nicki got sicker she eventually lost her ability to speak the correct words, and even though he continued to call her, she couldn't answer. After Nicki died, I sent the obituary to Matt, along with a letter telling him how important he was to her, and how he had given her joy during a difficult time in her life. But I always wondered if I should have picked up the phone and told Matt, so he wouldn't have been left wondering why she never called him. He could have come to visit her. I know that Nicki would have eventually found the right time to tell him, but unfortunately with her disease, things happened overnight, and once again her time ran out. As it turned out, a few years later Matt and I connected through Facebook, where he let me know that he was saddened to hear that Nicki died. He had very kind words to say about her, and that made me feel happy.

I thought back to the time I took Nicki to the eye doctor, and we chose not to have her eyes dilated because she had a reading to do. Later, we learned that brain tumors can sometimes be detected during dilation, and I wish that I had insisted she have a complete exam that day. I think Nicki may have actually been having some blurry vision at the time of her exam: though she asked if she could get glasses for reading, she never mentioned anything about problems with her vision. I asked her doctor if she really needed glasses with 20/20 vision, and he said that he didn't think so, but if she wanted a pair he would write a prescription. I bought her the glasses that day—but I wish with all my heart that I had not let her skip the dilation.

And there was one time when Nicki and I were attending a play at a local dinner theater. This was when Nicki had already started chemo. During the play, Nicki started to feel sick from her treatment, so during the intermission we went outside and walked to the side of the building because she had to vomit. There was an elderly man standing in the front of the theater smoking a cigarette, and when he heard that she was vomiting, he walked over and he said to her, "That's what you get for drinking. Best to lay off the booze." Obviously, he had no clue. I felt so bad for Nicki, who said nothing back to him. I didn't either, though—I just stood in front of her, trying to shield her until she stopped getting sick, and then we went home.

There were other similar incidents during her three-year battle with cancer, but we chose to concentrate on her happiness and not on confrontation. But now I wondered if I should have said something that evening. My daughter had *cancer*. Or when my husband filed divorce papers—all while our daughter was dying—why didn't I insist that my attorney put everything to do with the divorce off until my daughter's crisis was over? What was I *thinking*?

No. I just had to forgive myself, right here and right now. I had many regrets and felt remorse for some of my decisions, but I had always tried to make the right choices at the time and to do the right thing for Nicki. So now, I asked for God's forgiveness. I also asked for Nicki's, but in my heart, I knew that she had understood. The tumor had controlled everything: it forced her to stay in Jacksonville for treatments, hospital stays, procedures... *everything*. And at the time, I felt that our only hope was going to come from her doctors. I was relying completely on their expertise to save her life, and didn't want her to be far from them at any time in case something happened. But where was my faith?

And then it dawned on me: if I had let her travel and there had been problems, I would have had regrets about letting her go, just as I now had regrets about making her stay. I finally realized that I had done my best, or what I thought was best at the time. No one can do better than that, and so I forgave myself once again.

I was disappointed that none of Nicki's organs were considered viable for transplant because of all the chemotherapy and radiation she had received. Nicki had signed up to be an organ donor when she got her driver's license at sixteen, and when she knew that she had a fatal diagnosis, she made sure that her doctors were aware of her wishes. It would have felt good to know that a part of her was helping someone else to have a better quality of life, but it was not to be, so I let it go.

And then I thought about some of the things that I had done right. I was her mother. Taking care of her and nurturing her throughout her illness was naturally encoded in my DNA, but we also did fun things, too, that meant a lot to her—fun things that we could share together. On one special day, we went to the ocean to swim. Nicki and I spent two hours splashing each other in the water. The waves that day were so big that she lost her boogie board, and we had to go to Publix to buy another one. Then we went to the pool to get the salty water off of us; there, we floated on our rafts, almost falling asleep—we were both so tired. Even though we were exhausted from so many emotions, we still ended the day with a contest to see who could stay afloat without their raft longer. Nicki won the floating contest that day of course: she always won, because she tried the hardest. We were so happy, on this rare occasion that we weren't at the clinic, in the hospital, or facing a crisis. It was a week off from chemo, so we took the time to just have fun together, doing silly stuff and trying to forget—for a short while—the reality of what our life had become.

Then there was one time we went to the bookstore together. As we approached the checkout line, Nicki was distracted by a black sunglasses case stenciled with blue letters. The caption on the case read, "I would give up chocolate, but I'm no quitter." She picked it up, brought it to me, and announced, "I'm going to buy this." She had her own money, of course, but I knew that by bringing it to my attention, she was showing me just how strong her desire was to live. Nicki carried her black Ray Ban sunglasses in that case everywhere she went. She showed the same spontaneity the day she grabbed up a necklace in another store and said, "This is me, Mommy!" It had the Chinese character for "fearless" on it. Now, I use both of them, the sunglasses case and the necklace, reminding me that I'm no quitter, and I'm fearless, too. Nicki passed these gifts on to me, and they keep those memories fresh in my mind. I think that was what Nicki meant when she said, "Smile because it happened."

One thing that we all loved about Nicki was her ability to rise above her illness, her pain, and her sorrow, never letting cancer steal her creative instincts or her ability to smile under the worst of circumstances. When Nicki's grandparents gave her a camera for Christmas and she began photographing everything, I didn't realize it at the time but she was leaving me beautiful memories. I can still see her, grabbing her camera, and heading off to the beach for some photography. She knew her time was running out, and she wanted to make the most of it. Her doctors had already told her that they couldn't save her, and she needed to prepare herself to die. But that wasn't what Nicki wanted to do with the time she had left. She wasn't in denial; she was just going to live every day that she had left to its fullest. I can still hear her telling me, "Mommy, I have to follow my dreams." I loved how hard she worked to engage with her different passions.

As her disease progressed, she always made the most of the time God had given her. When she lost sight in her right eye, and then her ability to read, she never complained. We knew it was a losing battle when she lost her ability to speak, but she didn't feel that way—she just learned to sign. She used books on tape to finish school, because it was in her nature to always find a way to persevere. In the end, instead of graduating from college, Nicki was promoted to heaven. I thought about my friends who had reminded me that I gave her wings, not wanting to hold her back even though I was scared, and how I supported her decision to finish her freshman year of college—and to take her final exams when she was too sick to even be attending college. I did it because I loved her, and I knew how important it was to her.

That August, as I turned to walk home from the beach, a woman approached me, holding a beautiful shell, one without a blemish: a single oblong, brownish, smooth, shiny shell. I had never seen one like that. I asked her for the name of this perfect shell, and she told me, "I call it a brain shell. And this is the prettiest one I have ever found on this beach." She asked me to hold my hand out, and then, giving me the shell, gently closed my fingers over it. "Here," she said. "I want you to have it."

I didn't think much about it at the time, but now—a brain shell? She had to have been an angel sent by Nicki. I never saw her on the beach again, and I've spent a lot of time walking up and down that same stretch of beach. Where did she come from? That encounter was the moment Nicki gave me permission to let go of my regrets, just like I gave her permission to go into the arms of Jesus. It was over, and I knew that she had set me free. I forgave myself and walked home, feeling the warmth of Nicki's love.

SUNRISE

I knew that this was a path determined by God, since none of it was my choice or my doing. I had been confused why God hadn't answered my prayers for a miracle. Sure, I had accepted that Nicki was in heaven and would never feel pain again, but what was the purpose of taking her from me, from us? During those quiet months after her death, the long walks I took on the beach gave me time to talk with God—and to finally listen. I thought that, because I was a good, honest, and caring person who had spent my life thanking God for lending me two beautiful children, and for letting me live my dream of loving and raising my children, He wouldn't take my child from me. After all, I was a good mother.

In the months after Nicki's death, my dad's favorite song, "Alfie," by Burt Bacharach, kept running through my mind; I'd listened to it a lot when Nicki got sick, and thought of it often: "When you walk let your heart lead the way." When I finally decided to let my heart lead the way, I began to understand that I never really trusted God before now—I just thought I did. I told God what I wanted and what I wanted Him to do for me, but I never asked what I could do for Him—and never told Him that I would accept His will, no matter what. All that mattered to me was my happiness, and because Nicki was my joy, all I wanted was for her to live. When she became sick, I was consumed with my pain and the terrible thought of losing her. I didn't love God unconditionally: I loved my children more. I never said to God, "Let your will be done, not mine." I had asked God to heal Nicki, but never asked for the strength to let her go.

I've since learned that God allows tragedies to happen in life, but He is there to guide us through them and to help us pick up the pieces and make us whole again—if we allow Him in. In the late summer of 2005, I had reached that point, and was picking up the pieces of my life. I knew that I wanted to live with a sincere smile on my face once again, and to honor Nicki and make her proud. Some people would say that Nicki wouldn't even know, but *I* believe she knows, so it matters.

My immediate way to stay busy and embrace my future was to get to work on my house—and since it was almost twenty years old at this point, it needed a lot of help! I was afraid that I might lose the house in the divorce, and if that happened I didn't know where I would go: this had been our family's home for the past twelve years. I loved our neighbors, who had been there for us when Nicki was sick. Where would I go? I remember crying to my mom on the phone about it. She comforted me by saying, "Bunny, if you have to leave, it will be okay. A house is just a house, but you can make any house a home." My mom helped me understand that my joy had to come from inside of me, from very deep inside of me.

Fortunately, I was given first rights to buy the house, since Mike had moved out and purchased a condo without my knowledge. I was relieved when I was able to buy Mike out of his portion by relinquishing my share of our retirement funds, something that now I'm working on building back up. Unfortunately, the housing market was at its peak in 2006, so I had to pay Mike triple what we owed on our mortgage. But even though I lost a lot of the equity when the housing market fell, it was all mine now. My hope was to be strong and independent, and now I had a chance to be brave as well as healthy. I knew that I would have to make some changes in my life in order to move forward, and soon decided to make some tangible changes each day that I could look at in order to see progress. Money was tight after the divorce, but I now had control of my money; I planned carefully, and budgeted for ways to improve my physical surroundings, which I hoped would improve my mood and give me something substantial to do with my time.

When I purchased the house, I took some money from the loan so that I could make some home improvements. I started by having the tired, worn-out carpeting ripped up and replaced with hardwood floors. They certainly weren't top of the line, but at least they were wood! Then I had the shuttered windows dividing the kitchen from the sun porch removed, next painting all the walls a soft beige color to mellow things out and set a mood of peace and serenity.

Now, from my kitchen sink, I could better see the lake out back, which Nicki loved so much. I could commune with the ducks and turtles that Nicki had enjoyed photographing, along with bunnies, various water birds, and even an occasional bobcat. My kitchen was small, but I could enjoy the sound of the ocean anywhere in my house. The soothing waves and the ocean breeze continued to comfort me, helping me feel contentment as I began to rebuild my life.

Some things were emotionally hard for me to change, so I had to tuck the memories away in my mind and forget about them. While Nicki was sick, we had purchased a large La-Z Boy recliner couch for our family room; it was the most comfortable spot in our home for her, and it was a place where we could all be together: the four of us could fit on it, and we often ate our dinner there while watching football or something else on TV. But while I had an emotional attachment to it, the couch was no longer serving its purpose, and I felt lonely sitting on it by myself. Besides, it was the spot where Nicki had her first seizure, and it was way too big and heavy for my small beach house. So, I replaced it with a floral-patterned sofa with green leaves, white flowers, and dark brown stems, which resembled Nicki's favorite oleander tree in our neighborhood.

Now, the once-crowded room was open and light. I was literally and figuratively cleaning house and brightening up my environment. After my divorce, as my neighbors watched me carrying items out to the street, they smiled as they commented on how I seemed to be renewing my life. I would sit alone in my refreshed family room, with my journals and my computer on my lap, where I would write, listen to the waves, watch the wildlife outside, eat whole grain Goldfish crackers, and drink red wine: Goldfish were my comfort food when I was lonely, wine was my solace, and being alone was my protection from the world. I tried to eat a healthy diet, but it was sometimes a challenge to cook for myself. I started to run every day since I love running and knew how important it was for me, both physically and mentally.

Every morning, after sitting on my porch with a cup of coffee, I would head to the beach, Nicki's favorite place, and walk for hours; sometimes I ran. Nicki always loved the sunrise. Watching the spectacular array of colors each morning brought me close to her—and to God. The sunrise also reminded me that a new day was beginning, as was this new phase of my life.

*

One day, I called Nicki's fifth-grade teacher, Heather Nickodem. When Nicki died, Heather had written to me, sharing stories of her year with Nicki and telling me that, when I was ready, she would be glad to share some of Nicki's work that she had saved in classroom books. The time was right, so I called her and invited her over for lunch, as I felt I was now ready to go back and see more memories from Nicki. When Heather responded she was mysterious: "I'll bring you some treasures," she told me, "as long as you let me bring lunch, too. I have my reasons."

When she showed up at my house that afternoon, Heather was carrying a Longaberger picnic basket in one hand and what looked like a large picture frame, covered with a cloth, in the other. I gave her a big hug, and we went to sit on my sun porch, where I'd set a table for us to eat. In her basket, she had packed turkey sandwiches, apples, and various other fruits. After eating, I brought out my freshly baked brownies, the same ones I used to make for Nicki's fifth-grade class. At that point, Heather showed me something special about the picnic basket: it had been her class gift at the end of that school year, and inside the lid, each student had written a note and signed his or her name. When she asked me to open the lid, I saw it immediately, and a smile broke over my face: "You're the best! Nicki Leach." Both i's in Nicki was a star.

I told Heather how touched I had been years ago when she had called me, recommending Nicki for the gifted program. She had believed Nicki was academically advanced and that maybe she needed to be challenged a little more. With her recommendation, I did have Nicki tested, and let Heather know that the psychologist reported that Nicki was indeed bright, but most importantly, she was happy and seemed well-adjusted. He commented on how much she smiled, laughed, and enjoyed the interaction during testing. His recommendation was that she remain right where she was in school so that she could continue to perform at a comfortable and healthy pace, and so that she could keep smiling. I wholeheartedly agreed. It may make parents feel proud to advance their children in school or sports, but it can put stress on children to perform at an accelerated rate that may not be healthy for them. Heather understood when I told her this and said, "You left her where she was, because you wanted what was best for your child. I wish that all parents felt that way."

Next, she proceeded to share photographs of that class, including smiling pictures of Nicki, clips of Nicki in class videos, and Nicki's pages that she had pulled from class books. Heather had introduced journal writing in her class, and when she pulled out Nicki's journal I felt like heaven had sent me a gift. I had never seen many of these precious memories before. Together, Heather and I laughed, cried, and reminisced. I loved talking about my daughter, and I appreciated that she'd had such a wonderful teacher who played an important part in her life. Fifth grade had been Nicki's first year in public school, and I had been concerned that it might be hard to make a transition from the small church school that she had attended before. Mrs. Nickodem had ensured me that Nicki fit in perfectly, and her creative way of teaching, one that employed lots of acting and art, matched Nicki's learning style to a T.

Before Heather left my house, she said, "I have one

more special surprise for you." From behind her back she pulled out the large framed picture, which she dramatically unveiled to reveal some of Nicki's original artwork. I was completely taken aback when I saw a brilliant sunrise that I knew had been crafted by my Nicki's own delicate hands. Heather said that it was from a class book of haiku that the students had written and illustrated. It now hangs, framed, in my front hall. Under bright orange, red, and yellow semicircles is Nicki's seventeen-syllable Japanese poem:

> Rising from the ground
> Like a big, or'nge ball of fire,
> Sun lifting to sky.

Nicki surely had planned this meeting, and I was so touched with love that day. When Heather presented me with Nicki's haiku, I broke down in tears because it perfectly described the view from my kitchen windows. Whenever I pass it in the hall, I am reminded that each day is a new day, and I have a choice about where I spend it. Will it be in the past, the present, or the future?

I've gradually become okay with knowing that I will spend the rest of my life remembering the past, living in the present, and embracing the future. All three are important for healing and moving on. Just keep moving forward, I tell myself, but slowly—enjoying each day for what it brings. Keep smiling. As I breathe, I live. As I live, I remember. As I remember, I grieve. As I grieve, I think. As I think, I keep focusing on moving forward. It is what it is. I have to be healthy and whole. Having Nicki with me for nineteen years gave me the opportunity to be a great mother and friend. But now I am alone, and I need to concentrate on me. Now, I have a chance to strive to be a great person. Nicki made me want to be a better person, a stronger person. So, with my daughter in mind, I strive to become a person who embraces life once again—this time, with passion.

ONE FOOT IN FRONT OF THE OTHER

In Florida, school starts early every autumn. As I watched the neighborhood children standing on the sidewalk corner one late-August morning, waiting for the school bus on their first day of school, I choked back tears thinking of Nicki and Jesse at that age, excited about starting a new year. Jesse was now getting ready to start his senior year of college, and was long past the excitement of the bus stop. He didn't even live at home anymore. I had to remember that he was my only child now, and there was no one at home left to nurture except me.

I was spending most of my time in solitude, inside my house or on the beach. I thought it was important that I try to spend some time around people now, but I wanted something fresh and new. One of the stipulations of the divorce agreement was that Mike would have to finance the rest of my college education if I chose to pursue it. Why not? I thought. Do I have any other plans right now? Besides, I wouldn't mind hanging around the UNF campus. It would certainly make me feel close to Nicki's memory. I'd already spent a lot of time there—of course, I was mostly in the parking lot, but maybe I should check it out.

So, one day, I hopped in the car and drove over to the campus; it seemed like by this point my car knew the way by heart. I was surprised to find that my psychology courses from various colleges in Michigan would transfer, and after two years of study at UNF, I could become a grief counselor. Maybe this was my new mission in life? Maybe my place was to counsel people who were going through what I had been—and was still going—through. I just hoped that I wouldn't embarrass my son if I ran into him between classes.

And thus there I was, at fifty years old, back in college with twenty-year-olds. I wasn't sure how I would keep up with them, but I really didn't care. I just didn't know what else to do, and I found that I related better to this age group than people my own age, especially ever since Nicki had become sick. I had been completely wrapped up in Nicki's world for so long that now I couldn't let go of her surroundings. I had to go back and embrace it on my own. I remembered what Nicki's math professor, Joe Flowers, wrote about Nicki after hearing that she had died: "How sad—she was so young and beautiful, courageous and intelligent. She was by far the best and brightest student in my class."

A month into my new college experience, I found myself confronted with October 3, which would have been Nicki's twentieth birthday. The previous year, she and I had driven to the mall so she could make a Build-a-Bear. On our way home, we had passed by UNF and seen Jesse's white jeep traveling in the left lane on the highway. We chuckled because he always drove in the left lane to avoid the merging traffic from the right. We got right behind his car and followed him until he saw us in the rear view mirror, then pulled up beside him. As we did, Nicki put her orange bear out the window and made it dance for him. Jesse was always serious while driving, but this time he couldn't contain himself and started cracking up with laughter.

So, Jesse and I decided that this year we would go to the mall and build another bear for Nicki. We picked out a brown bear, a long blonde wig, a sparkly, silver fairy outfit, and a shiny red satin heart to put inside our Nicki-bear.

Then we stuffed the bear, rubbed its heart, and made a wish. Our last mission was to go into the bathroom with a recording chip, where we sang "Happy Birthday" to Nicki. Our bear keeper put the chip into our bear's paw, inserted our red satin heart into the bear's chest, then sewed it up. We took our bear and headed to Nicki's favorite restaurant for lunch. With raised glasses filled with bubbly champagne, we toasted our favorite girl, and ordered her favorite dessert, Bananas Foster.

I was so happy that Jesse was available to share Nicki's birthday with me that first year, but I also realized that I couldn't expect Jesse to accompany me every year to celebrate, so the next year I started a new tradition: since Ryan had always sent Nicki roses for her birthday, I decided that I would buy myself a huge bouquet of roses each year to put on my dining room table to remind me of Nicki's special day. I would treasure the memories of birthdays past: the day she was born when she wrapped her tiny hand around my finger; her first birthday when she dove into her cake face-first, and the way she used to love to jump on her Barbie balloons to pop them. I didn't want to be sad: I wanted to celebrate her life.

But the pain was still there, and both Thanksgiving and Christmas in 2005 were very sad. I thought it would be okay to let myself go deeply into my grieving, loneliness, and sorrow; in fact, I thought it might be healthy to get it all out right then. On Thanksgiving, Jesse and I went to the Sawgrass Marriott at the TPC, which had been a tradition for years in our family, one started by Nicki. We would get all dressed up and, after our meal, we would walk the beautiful grounds, admiring the waterfalls and bridges, before asking someone to take our family Christmas photo.

So this year, before eating our Thanksgiving meal, Jesse and I said a special prayer asking Nicki to pray for us; we knew that she didn't need our prayers anymore. After our meal, we walked the surrounding grounds where Jesse used to chase his little sister after Thanksgiving dinner. We were sad, but thankful that we had each other. Before leaving, we asked someone to take our photo together, just like usual.

Christmas was even harder because I didn't want to call to ask Jesse to go get me a fresh tree. He had helped me in so many ways, and I wanted to stop asking him to do everything for me now: I had to learn how to make it alone. So I went to Ace Hardware and bought a fake tree; then, at home, I brought down from the attic the many boxes of ornaments that went back over twenty years, mostly ornaments that Jesse and Nicki had made at school or church for me every year. Then there were the ornaments that I had made from our Thanksgiving photos, twenty-three in all. I decorated the tree just like I had all the previous years, but this year—of course—was different. When Jesse came over on Christmas Day, he walked over to the tree and looked at all the ornament photos of our once-whole family of four. He looked sad, so I walked over and hugged him, but there was nothing to say—our tears said it all. Having him there to grieve with me, and knowing that we would share memories and stories of Nicki for the rest of our lives, helped so much and gave me comfort.

The following year, I decorated my tree with butterflies, but in fact I haven't put a tree up since then. I realized that since it made me sad, I simply wouldn't do it, and if I ever decide to decorate a tree again, I probably won't pull out the family ornaments. But, I still keep them in boxes in the attic for Jesse, if he ever wants to decorate his own tree with them.

Because it became difficult to communicate with Nicki when she was unable to speak, and since I now had a newfound compassion for others, I took American Sign Language classes as one of my electives at UNF. I especially enjoyed the lab component because I got to interact with other students in a small group setting. This gave me the opportunity to share stories about Nicki, and was my way to get to know some of my classmates on a more personal level. I have to admit, I was happy in school, and finally in my element.

My psychology classes, particularly Life Span Development, brought a tremendous amount of deep grieving out in me, and I was thankful that my professor was available to meet with me on a regular basis. My social psychology class wasn't too painful, especially when, after the semester was over, my professor asked me out on a date. But Life Span made it hard to sit in class without secretly crying. Several times, my professor let me leave the classroom while watching films about stages of development from conception to old age. Knowing that Nicki didn't live to see old age, let alone her twenties, saddened me to no end. And, studying DNA was especially confusing, because all I could do was wonder how Nicki had developed a brain tumor in the first place.

Overall, the UNF experience gave me another platform for my grief, a way to meet new people, and a place to hide from my community for a while. I tried to blend in and look normal but, like Nicki, I knew I was different. It took a year at UNF before I figured out that I didn't want to be a grief counselor after all. Staying mired down in others' grief wasn't what I wanted to do with the rest of my life; I wanted to move forward, honoring Nicki's request to "Be happy, Mommy."

One day, while sorting through my mail, I felt a chill go through me when I saw at a flyer advertising a 5K race for breast cancer. It was the pink ribbon in particular that grabbed my attention. The year before, another similar flyer had arrived, and I had tossed it in the garbage, hardly giving it a glance. Nicki had been watching me, as she was always curious about the daily mail—she was used to getting a lot of cards and messages of good wishes, which she loved. I could feel her eyes on me, and when I tossed the pink ribbon brochure in the trash, she spoke up. "What was that, Mommy?" I shook my head and said, "It's nothing." She knew what it was, though, and said, "Let me see it." I didn't care about other people's cancer at the time; I was only concerned with my daughter's disease. And besides, Nicki had a brain tumor, not breast cancer.

But still, I pulled the brochure out of the trash, telling her, "It's for a race for breast cancer. I don't run." She said, "You can walk it, Mommy. I have cancer. Your dad died from cancer. Please don't throw that away. You can do something to help. I know you can walk it. You just put one foot in front of the other, and, to run? Well, you just do it faster." Oh, how she had opened my eyes that day—but I had quickly forgotten about it. I was so caught up in her final months of life, and then my months of grieving, that I had forgotten that there was something I could do. I suddenly felt so selfish to think that my daughter's cancer was all that mattered. *Everyone's* suffering mattered.

So, I started signing up for races. At first I walked them—just putting one foot in front of the other, like I was doing in my daily life—but before long, I was running. I ran every charity race available during the next year, running them while thinking about everyone with cancer. I knew that my nickels, my dimes, my dollars, and my sweat were contributing to help find a cure for cancer so that someday, someone would not have to go through what Nicki—and the rest of our family—had gone through. I thought about those people who were still fighting for their lives, and about Nicki watching me from above, knowing that I had kept my word.

I remembered our discussions about how I could help others with cancer. About a year into her cancer treatment, Nicki had become very concerned for the lives of other young adults with cancer. She didn't know anyone her age that had cancer, and I wished that she had—but we were so busy, in and out of the hospital, treatment, and school, that she just was never able to meet anyone like her. When she was diagnosed at seventeen, all her friends were healthy, and many of them couldn't understand her new life. Even Nicki herself didn't know the suffering that came with cancer until it struck her. It was then that she became aware of the isolation it often caused. She had even talked with Dr. Pitel, at the children's clinic, about wanting to move to the adult clinic, because she was so uncomfortable among the clowns—to cheer up patients—and little children. She felt isolated from her peers and wanted to address this situation. She wanted her voice heard before her time ran out.

That's why she had asked me to help. Nicki knew she couldn't be the only one going through this, and she truly cared about others; she kept telling me that I could help other people who had cancer, but I didn't know how. Nicki always reminded me that because I now knew just how isolated teenagers and college students could be because of all their hospital stays and treatments, I could find some way to help. "Mommy, you can do something to help others like me who have cancer," she would say. "You can see how it is for me." I've always tried to help others, and I have a deep passion for all people who are suffering. Watching Nicki battle cancer broke my heart, especially when I saw other teenagers and young adults with the disease. I kept thinking about our conversations and of the ways that I might help her age group, especially students who had cancer.

So, while running one of the races, it hit me—just before I crossed the finish line, the answer came to me. I wasn't sure yet how I was going to do it, or how it would work, but I knew what it was: I was going to start a foundation.

At this point, I realized that my school assignments just weren't as important as the assignment Nicki had left for me, and now was the time to honor it. After running in dozens of races for cancer, I was now ready to impact teenagers and young adults in a more direct way. So on January 1, 2006, I created the Nicki Leach Foundation, an organization that would offer scholarships to young adults with cancer. Keeping my daughter's memory alive and honoring her was important to me; this foundation would be her final gift to other teenagers and young adults, not mine.

I knew from Nicki's experience that Dreams Come True, a local organization that grants wishes to children that have life-threatening illnesses, as well as the national Make-A-Wish Foundation, only offer assistance up to the age of seventeen or eighteen years old. And in fact, Nicki had turned down her offer from Dreams Come True, saying she already had all that she wanted: her family, good friends, college, and her camera. She asked the organization to give her wish to someone really sick, because at the time she felt that she was doing okay.

I also knew that older teens and college students didn't usually want to go on dream vacations or receive a visit with someone famous. This was the in-between generation: not children, but not quite adults. Mostly, they were in high school or college at this age. Although I was prepared for the foundation to receive requests for money for wigs or new wardrobes, to accommodate rapid body changes, I knew from Nicki that most recipients might just want money for college expenses or car maintenance, or even mounting bills. Mostly, I knew they'd want the help so that they could continue on with their lives as normally as possible.

The first thing that I did was to build a website with photos and Nicki's story. Next, I contacted a professional web-hosting company, met with the owner, and showed him my ideas so that he could host us and so we could collect donations. Once we had the website up and running, I found an accountant who helped us file for our 501(c)(3) status, which would establish the foundation as a charitable cause. Little did I know that, in order to obtain this status, the foundation had to first have a board of directors, including a chairman. So I called up Nicki's oncologist, Dr. Paul Pitel, who graciously agreed, saying, "I would do anything for Nicki." As difficult as it all sounded, we had a board of directors in place within a week. I was thrilled as to how helpful and supportive everyone was. After the paperwork was complete, I began getting our fundraising ideas in order while we waited about six months until we were granted our charitable status. Once that was set, the applications started pouring in—even before we had the money!—but it all evened out in the end.

There are a few requirements to be eligible to receive a grant from Nicki's foundation: applicants need to fill out some necessary forms; then, they must write a letter telling us how cancer has changed their lives and how they would use their monetary gift from Nicki. After the foundation's first year, I knew that Nicki had been right: eighty percent of our applicants wanted money for college expenses, and the remaining twenty percent wanted help with their bills. They just wanted to continue on with their lives as normally as possible.

I will never forget the day we received our first request for assistance. I was so happy that our system was working and that our young adults had found us. I quickly opened the envelope and found myself looking directly into the eyes of a beautiful young woman. From her photo attached to the application, I could tell that she had already been through so much in her young life. As I read her letter, I began to tear up.

Dear Bunny,

Originally from Valley City, ND, I moved to Fargo, ND, in the fall of 2005 to begin my life as a college student in pursuit of obtaining a Bachelor's degree in Business Management. Since that time I have taken classes at NDSU, MSUM and MSCTC.

During my freshmen year at NDSU I realized the campus was just too big for me, so fall of 2006 I transferred to MSUM and MSCTC. I was really looking forward to the beginning of a new year, on a smaller campus. I registered for fall classes, and it seemed to me the change to a smaller environment was a better fit, so I then registered for spring semester. Spring semester started as quickly as it ended. Here's my story...

February 3, 2007, I was invited to attend a social outing with some friends. About 11 p.m. I began experiencing a "different" feeling, one that I'd never experienced before, so decided it would be best to end the night early.

In the early morning hours of February 4, I found myself lying in an emergency room bed at Merit Care Hospital in Fargo, unsure of the events that brought me there. My parents arrived within

25 minutes of receiving a call from my boyfriend who had described what he thought was a seizure. After several tests it was determined that I had a brain tumor and would require surgery.

On February 6, I underwent major brain surgery in which the surgeon felt he was able to remove the entire tumor. I didn't get to go home and come back for the surgery. I was in the hospital for a week and didn't know what was to come. A few days following, the biopsy revealed very unwelcome news. News I'd always hoped I wouldn't hear in my lifetime. Cancer! I was diagnosed with glioblastoma multiforme stage 4 and was told by the doctor that I had a one in five chance of survival. At this point my mom was balling; I had to say to her: "Mom! Stop crying; I'm not crying. Now stop it, I'm going to get through it, and I'm strong enough for us all. Everything is going to work out in the end." I would sometimes think to myself that there was a decent chance of me getting cancer with it being prevalent in family history (Dad's side: Dad, Dad's sister, Dad's mother, Dad's niece, and Dad's aunt). With my family having such a strong history of cancer, I knew the road ahead would be challenging and uncertain at times. I remained under the care of the hospital staff for several days, and then returned to my family home in Valley City so that I could receive round the clock medical care. At this time, I was in the middle of a move to a new apartment, so luckily for my family, mostly everything was already packed. After being out of the nest for two years, I didn't like the idea of going back to live with Mom and Dad.

Mid February I began daily treatments and 60-mile one-way trips to Fargo for radiation and chemotherapy. I began to lose my hair after the fourth week of radiation. I then demanded that I go shopping to get a wig, within the next two days. Not having hair was a major obstacle for me, quite emotional. A girl loves to have hair to style, and without it, this wasn't possible. Even with the wig, I was limited. I needed this ASAP because I was still an active college student who was just on medical leave from classes!

So, Grandma and I went wig shopping and she bought one for me! One thing that I realized after losing my hair was that it was something that I always took for granted. Also, not being able to drive "for a year" due to a seizure was even harder for me. I didn't think that being able to have the freedom of going where I want, when I want was so valuable. Lucky for me, I was given my driving privileges back about a month ago, and I love every minute of it. I often remind myself how convenient it is. However, paying for the gas and insurance is something I don't miss. I look back at the pictures that were taken days before my diagnosis and realized that my hair wasn't as bad as I thought. My hair is growing back now and I am now able to go without the wig OR bandana. I wore a bandana daily for a good five months.

In June 2007 I didn't want to put my education on hold for any longer, so I decided to go back to college this semester. I am only a part-time student, but the classes are challenging for me. I now realize that I probably wasn't ready to go back yet, but I am not the kind of person to just sit around and let cancer rule my life. While my cancer remains a health concern now, and quite possibly into my future, I believe that keeping my life as normal as possible will be my best treatment in restoring my health. Keeping normal to me means resuming my studies while keeping up with my social life.

Overall, I have been asked many questions about my struggles with cancer, but more comments about my personality as well. Everyone wonders how I still look so good. I tell them that I am just trying to stay as normal as possible and keep up my appearance as well as I can. I don't like it when people see me on my bad days because they feel bad for me, and I don't want that. Everyone asks me how I keep such a normal life and not look down on the fact that I am living with cancer. I continue to tell them, "Cancer is not a death sentence. I'm not going to let it run my life. I am going to get through it. For now it's just a bump in the road that God has placed upon me. I'm going to beat this thing and live to tell my story for years to come."

Lindsay Sauer

Typically, after our review board approves an application, I send out an e-mail with the good news and to verify the applicant's contact information.

This was Lindsay's response to my congratulatory e-mail:

Dear Bunny,

It is with a grateful heart of appreciation that I am responding to your most welcomed e-mail indicating your special interest in providing financial assistance toward my upcoming college expenses.

My family Mom, Dad, younger sister and I, have each visited The Nicki Leach Foundation website and were all touched by Nicki's legacy. We agree that Nicki's story very much relates to what I am currently experiencing in my own life. Attached are a few pictures of me taken prior to and during treatment.

Currently a junior, I plan to attend classes at Minnesota State Community and Technical College Moorhead this fall and then transfer credits to Minnesota State University Moorhead where I will finish with a bachelor's degree in business. The community and technical college do not offer dormitory living. Therefore I am required to obtain apartment living, which is an added expense to me. Because I will be on maintenance chemotherapy for a good portion of the school year, I am not able to take a full class load and I am unable to secure part-time employment. The cost of tuition and books for fall semester is approximately $1,200 for tuition and $250 for books.

Thank you again for your help and I look forward to any additional assistance you may be able to provide me as I work through this difficult time in my life.

"Smile because it happened."

Sincerely, Lindsay Sauer

It has been both an honor and a challenge for me to run the Nicki Leach Foundation in memory of my daughter. Even though I know that our young adults have life-threatening cancer, I hadn't thought about how I would handle it emotionally if one of our young adults died, especially after everything I experienced with Nicki's death. The first time it happened, I called my mom, crying my eyes out.

She simply said to me, "Bunny, I know this is very hard for you, but this is what Nicki wanted you to do, and you have to be strong. Focus on the good side, which is helping these young people when they need it the most. If they don't survive cancer, keep in mind that they are at peace, and not suffering anymore. And when they get to heaven, Nicki is there to show them around."

In the past three years, many of our young adults have passed on from various forms of cancer: breast, colon, bone, brain... every kind that adults get, and even some new and unexplainable forms. It's heartbreakingly sad, but I have to be strong to do this work. In fact, I often get letters and phone calls from mothers who just want to talk, seeking someone else with the same experience. I'm so proud of these young adults who have cancer and how open they are, and I enjoy exchanging emails and conversations on the phone with them as well. I'm so thankful that we're here for them and able to help out when they need us. These teenagers and young adults are much deserving and most often overlooked. We want to continue to help them in any way we can, and to put smiles on the faces of teenagers and young adults who have cancer.

APRIL

I was born in the diamond month of April, on Easter Sunday fifty-one years ago. It had always been a happy month for me: my mother was born in April; spring comes in April; and, it's a holy time of year. These were joyful events. My beloved daughter passed away in April—one year ago. From then on, it would always be a mournful month for me. Yet, I don't want April to sadden me; I want it to excite me. Spring is when I open my windows to smell the air full of sweetness from the roses planted in my back yard. I listen to the waves from the Atlantic Ocean gently rush to shore, and the salty breeze moistens my skin after the dry winter season. I love everything about this time of year, especially memories of walking on the beach with Nicki, and jumping together into the crisp, briny water.

For a while, I had been able to forget what my life had become. The first year after Nicki's passing had been very difficult, because it was filled with notable days that were especially hard to acknowledge without her: her birthday, Thanksgiving, Christmas, even the first Valentine's Day (my wedding anniversary) without her, or simply the thought of how we spent the last one. And, of course, April 29, the day that she died. Those days would always leave a hole in my heart, because she's no longer here to celebrate with me—and never will be again. It might get a little easier year by year, but not much. And no matter what, every April 29 will forever be somber.

I sometimes think about my birthday in 2006, when Nicki treated me to dinner, and how I memorized her precious hands—hands that could, at the time, barely sign her name. I missed her so much, yet I was thankful that she had been delivered from her pain and distress. Although it was painful to watch her that day, she left me with a memory of her love, and that special day will continue to warm my heart every April 5, though it will also bring tears to my eyes every year that I celebrate a birthday without her here. Thankfully, they tore down the Ruby Tuesday in our town a year after her passing—I guess Nicki didn't want me driving by it every day and feeling sad, since I had promised her that I would be happy. Eventually the Ruby Tuesday was gone and replaced with another one of her favorite restaurants, Chick-fil-A, for which I was thankful. Our girl loved to eat. This was yet another reminder for me to keep moving forward and not to go back to the sad memories from my past. Even though Nicki isn't with me on earth now, she's still with me in memory and spirit.

The first year after Nicki's death, when April 29 rolled around, I started the day by walking to Nicki's favorite place, the beach. She was right: big orange sunrises over the Atlantic Ocean are more beautiful than anything, especially this time of year. Later that day, since it was the anniversary of Nicki's passing, Father Ted wanted to bless her resting spot at the cemetery. Since the cemetery was a new addition to the grounds of the church, Nicki was the only one buried there. One year earlier, Mike, Jesse, and I had walked with Father Ted through these woods to pick out our Nicki's resting place; the woods were so thick it was hard to pick her spot. Father Ted had the blueprints of the land and guided us to what would be the middle of the cemetery, and helped us choose the perfect piece of land to lay her to rest. I had always loved the sound of church bells, and hoped that Nicki would hear them when they rang.

For the anniversary blessing, I sent invitations to family and friends, as well as the wonderful people in our community who helped and supported us when she was sick, inviting them to come gather in her memory. It was a beautiful spring day, and I was happily surprised when, one by one, they all came carrying baskets of fresh flowers. We sang songs, prayed, and honored her "Memory Eternal." All the sacred traditions of the Orthodox Church were comforting and made for a blessed occasion. After the blessing, Jesse and I went out for dinner, and later I spent the rest of the day thinking and writing—not about her last day, but about the good times we'd had with her.

Looking out over the lake now as I write, and at the Guana Preserve from my back porch window, I see a raptor, soaring through the sky. Straining to see if it's an eagle, I follow it until it is out of my view. I think for a second that I should run and grab my camera like Nicki would have. But I stop myself, and simply take in the view for now. I'm trying to make new memories these days.

When I think about Nicki's photographs, I see all the beauty she captured with just one eye—she had such a gift! Her new passion had become my lasting joy. When Nicki began photographing the beauty of this world, she must have known that she would never return in her physical body to see this earth again. So her camera became her constant companion the last year of her life; she held on to it as if it were a best friend. At the time, I didn't realize that she would be leaving me this gift, such beautiful memories of our times spent together, visions of her private solitude, her peaceful times spent in nature, capturing memories, leaving them behind. I hope that others will enjoy the beauty she captured while saying good-bye to this earthly planet. It makes me think that if God gave us so much beauty here, it must be spectacular in Heaven.

One of my favorites of Nicki's photos is the colorful picture of the turtle in the road, though it's the story behind the photo that will always mean so much to me. At the time, I didn't even realize Nicki was so gifted with her camera. I could see that it gave her so much happiness during a time when her life was slipping away, as well as a new goal to achieve; slowly, she was reaching the end, like the turtle's pace through life. Another of my favorites is one of an oleander; this particular tree is in our neighborhood, and we must have passed by it a thousand times when we walked to the beach together. Sometimes, when Nicki was sick, I would see the tree and silently cry, fearing that one day I would have to pass by it without her—or, rather, that I would need to learn how to survive apart from her. We never really talked about it much; we wanted to live in the moment. Once we were forced to confront the reality that she could die, we were finally able to embrace the present. We were living to enjoy every day we were given, leaving the future in the hands of God. She had just been getting ready to leave the nest when we found out what was wrong with her, and it would take a miracle for her future plans and dreams to come true now that everything had changed. But cancer could never take away her love for her family, friends, and the beauty of this God-created earth. She had embraced so much, and photography was her last adventure. Her camera gave her peace, I could see that; so, I named her collection "A Peaceful Journey."

Although Nicki wasn't famous, and never got the chance to travel far from home, she cherished what she had: her time here with me—with us—even if it was short.

We never take anything with us when we pass on from this earth, but we can leave so much behind, such as memories for loved ones to hold onto, and legacies that will last a lifetime. Once, I looked forward to being the mother of the bride, and thought that if Nicki ever gave birth I would be right beside her, excited to become a grandmother. I had the same hopes and desires that all parents have for their children. Now, though, I would be happy just to see my daughter again. I will always hold on to that hope.

But April 2005 was more shattering than anything I had experienced in my fifty years on this earth. The timing of her death in that beautiful month of April—always my favorite—three weeks after my birthday and one day before her grandmother's seventieth birthday, was mystifying. My mother was nineteen when she had me, so I found it eerie that her granddaughter died at that same age.

Losing a child is the most traumatic event that can happen to a parent. I wish to honor my daughter's passing by not being angry, and especially by not giving up. I wanted both of my children to know God when they were very young, and they did. That was my biggest hope in life, the most important reality that I know. I choose to believe in God, and will always picture Nicki in God's arms, where she is protected, loved, and safe. I want to see my daughter again, and have faith that we will unite once again in Heaven. I will do nothing to lose that chance. I'm excited, now, holding onto the knowledge of what I have to look forward to when I die: seeing Nicki beautiful, whole, and without disease. Just knowing that I will hold her once again, and that she will know me, sustains me. We will be together once more, embracing the promise of eternity, never suffering again. This much I know.

ROSES

That spring, something unexpected happened: a new man came into my life.

It was Priscilla, Nicki's voice teacher, who brought us together. She was a good friend of Roberts wife, and thought we should meet. In fact, it was only about four months after his wife had died from cancer, and eight since Nicki's passing; Priscilla, thinking that, since we had both recently lost a loved one, we might keep each other company and work through our grief together, invited us over to her house for dinner. He was a prominent, wealthy man in our community who was much respected for his kindness and helpfulness to others—in all, a very well respected gentleman. We hit it off right away, and soon were able to share in our grief and provide companionship to one another during a lonely time. It may have been too soon for us to date, and even though it was nice having someone in my life again, I was still grieving for Nicki, and couldn't truly give my heart to anyone at this time. But, I believe that we both served as compassionate companions for each other since we had both lost a loved one and our spouses. I was so alone at that time and it felt good to have someone to do things with.

During this time, Jesse graduated from college. I was so proud of my son, considering all that he endured during his four years of college. Jesse was as determined as Nicki, and graduated *summa cum laude*. I was still grieving so hard for Nicki, and couldn't believe she wasn't here to see her brother graduate—she would have been so proud of him too. After graduation, Jesse took a job in Savannah and moved away. Secretly, I wanted him to stay, and cried for months after he moved; I missed him and wanted him to be close to make up for lost time with him. But he had already given so much of himself to us, and I knew I couldn't ask him for anything more—it wasn't fair. We both had to live our lives independently. Jesse had helped me so much after Nicki died, and I would miss him terribly, but in my heart I knew that he wanted to live his life as a young man with independence: he needed to do what he wanted and finally go off on his own. So, even though it was extremely hard to see him go, I supported him with his freedom.

However, having someone new in my life at this time made it that much easier to watch my son leave to lead his own life. I was slightly overwhelmed with home renovations, too, so it was a bonus to have an accomplished businessman who was also handy with tools. There was still a lot to do around the house, and the timing couldn't have been better. He immediately started helping me with all the work that needed to be done. He missed having a woman to do things for, and I was glad to be available! When I was young, my dad had always known his way around a tool bench, and I had fond memories of watching him fix my bike when I was a young girl and, as I got older, my car. I had always been able to count on him, and now I had a man to count on once again.

He also helped me with some minor updates in my kitchen by tiling the walls above my countertops with leftover travertine marble from a project in his house—he even set a saw up in my yard and cut the tiles to fit just the way I had designed. One of my favorite things about my house is the long cement walkway that leads from the street to my front door; he replaced that with slate, then put a path made of butterfly-shaped stepping-stones from my front door to the driveway. I didn't have to spend very much money, and, because frankly I didn't have much money to spend, he helped out with expenses, paying for some of the repairs and shopping with me at warehouses and garage sales to stay within my budget. He also sometimes would use leftover materials from his own projects and would ask for scraps left at job sites in the neighborhood. One time we saw a light fixture by the side of the road, so we stopped and picked it up, took it home, and refurbished and spray-painted it—now, it's hanging in my dining room! I was so thankful that he was willing to help because at the time, I don't know how I could have done it alone. Though he'd retired early, he owned a golf course landscaping business, so he could borrow trucks and personnel, which we used to help finish our church's new cemetery and to complete the landscaping around Nicki's grave. He was a dream come true.

He had a rose garden in his back yard, and would often pick a bouquet of colorful roses and surprise me with them at my door. I would get so excited about each rose because I loved to smell their different fragrances. Each rose meant something special to me. He would laugh at me because I even named them. I called the red ones "love roses," because they have a deep, rich color—like velvet—intense and passionate. The yellow roses smelled sweet and smooth like the sun dripping honey crème. The white ones smelled pure and innocent, like angels flying through clouds, or whipped cream on top of fresh strawberries. Orange roses were fun, playful, and a bit flirty. They smelled like orange peel, zesty and fresh, like orange marmalade.

But my favorite rose of all is the pink rose, softly saying "It's a girl." Pink roses are youthful, flirty, and fun, a bit shy but still confident, playful but delicate, yet not to be undermined because of their feminine nature. All of these were the traits my Nicki had. When I put a bouquet together in her memory, I embrace her witty spirit, then take a deep breath and smell the roses, breathing in her smell, the one that I will never forget for eternity. When she died, I grabbed all of her clothes and buried my nose in them. I couldn't breathe deeply enough to bring her back to life, but I tried. Now, the pink roses helped.

FOLLOW YOUR HEART

I made it over another hurdle the day I went with my friend to watch one of her students perform in a local dance recital. Nicki had started dancing at four years old, and I'd watched her dance for the next twelve years—tap, ballet, lyrical, and jazz. Sitting in the auditorium, watching all the little ballerinas on stage in their sequined, fluffy costumes, brought back so many memories. I smiled; I had recently given away all of Nicki's costumes. I couldn't have done that a year ago, let alone sit in this auditorium. But now I could feel them coming—tears. Secretly taking a tissue from my purse, I dabbed my eyes, thankful that it was dark in this auditorium. While I thought through my memories of Nicki, I started talking with her in my mind. All the little girls had buns in their hair; I had put Nicki's hair up in a bun so many times—I still had our box of bobby pins in my bathroom drawer. I was just getting started down memory lane when I heard her voice: "Be happy, Mommy." Then I saw a vision of her dancing on stage, twirling, floating like an angel. My heart ached, but I was so filled with joy. Once again, she had made me smile.

As I sat mesmerized by the atmosphere in the dimly lit theater, watching the sparkly costumes and listening to the music, I couldn't stop reminiscing; in my mind, I saw Nicki grow from a toddler to a teenager. I remembered how much she liked watching the "babies" dance: at every one of her recitals, she would sit in the auditorium watching the little ones perform, waiting until the last minute to go backstage to get ready for her dance. She would have enjoyed watching this recital—she loved to teach young children. During the summer of her freshmen year in high school, she got her dream job teaching acting and dance at a local performing arts theater in Atlantic Beach, making fifty dollars a week. Her students were between five and ten years old, and they really looked up to Nicki, even though she was only fourteen herself.

One of my favorite videos of Nicki is one from that summer, at the recital performance of the children Nicki taught. In it, Nicki is dressed in a black leotard, flapping bright yellow wings as she moves around the stage, guiding the little ones in their own butterfly outfits. Perhaps Nicki is teaching little children in heaven now, children who were also called by God to leave their mothers too soon. From what I know about heaven, it's very possible.

I left the theater feeling happy, having completed another step in my journey to be happy and at peace once again.

One thing that I had to remember was that this new man in my life was grieving too: he'd recently lost his wife who he loved. They had often enjoyed traveling together, and he missed going on trips since his wife died. There were so many places he wanted to revisit, and he wondered if I would accompany him down his own memory lane, and make new memories together. He had given so much to me and walked beside me through so many memories of my own, and now I had the opportunity to help him in return. I hadn't traveled much since my husband retired from professional tennis fifteen years before, and I sometimes wished that we could have traveled together later in life. But I had to get over that way of thinking. I was ready to travel again, and thought that seeing new places might take my mind off living alone in the house.

Soon I was going to exciting places, like New York, Carmel, California, and British Columbia, where I was able to enjoy the local culture and sights. He also took me to Boston, Seattle, Montana, and back to my hometown in Grass Lake, Michigan, where I hadn't been in over twenty years. My grandmother was ninety years old now and still living in the same house where I used to visit her as a child. My grandpa had died soon after burying his son, my dad, and Grandma never remarried. While my sister Lynn and her daughters, Justina and Dawn, as well as my best friend Terri, had come to Nicki's funeral, I didn't get to visit with them at that time. Now, though, I wanted to go back home to Michigan, and spend some time reuniting with them. I wanted to see where I used to work, and visit with some of those friends, too. I had always planned to take Nicki and Jesse back home to show them where I grew up—indeed, where they had been born. I thought we had the rest of our lives to do that, but we didn't. I still hope to take Jesse one day. With all his artsy talents, I know he'll love Ann Arbor. I cried a lot going back the first time, because I realized how much I really had missed my dad, but was so thankful that my new friend loved to travel and took me back home to see my grandma, my sister and her girls, and my friends. It was a trip I'll always cherish.

There came a time when I felt ready to spend some time away from home and take a trip by myself, so I drove to the Blue Ridge Mountains in North Carolina. My friend and former tennis partner owned a home overlooking Grandfather Mountain, and, as she knew the trauma that

I'd been through, she asked if I would like to go to her cabin and take care of her two dogs for a week while she and her husband went to a wedding. She knew it would be a peaceful getaway for me. So I said, why not? I knew it would be fun to get away, and I'd been pet-sitting to earn a little extra money I could spend.

One day I drove into Boone for lunch and some shopping. Although I wasn't quite sure why, I decided to wander into a quaint little yarn shop. Its window boxes caught my eye: they were painted canary-yellow and filled with an array of violet, pink, fuchsia, and white Gerber daisies. I now think that Nicki was guiding me inside: she knew how much I loved to knit during her illness, and how much comfort it gave me. I remembered all the hats, scarves, blankets, and purses that I had knitted for her, especially her favorite, a book bag made with European wool in forest green, that she used to carry her school books in at college.

A friendly bell rang when I opened the door. Sitting on a high stool behind a counter was a slender, middle-aged woman with curly brown hair. She was knitting—of course—and was wearing a navy blue knitted sweater. I was impressed, as I'd never knitted a sweater.

"What brings you in today?" she asked. I was the only one in the store. "Oh, I just wandered in to look around," I said. "Your shop caught my eye, and your flowers looked so inviting. I used to love to knit, but I stopped."

"Why in the world did you stop?" She smiled, tilting her head to the side, while peeking over the top of her silver reading glasses.

"My daughter was sick for three years. I started knitting because it was so relaxing, and it gave me something to do during hospital stays and clinic visits. I stopped when she died."

When she heard that, she got up off the stool, came around the counter, wrapped her arms around me, and gave me a big hug. Then she asked for the whole story. I guess it was the environment that set it off, but I began to cry as I told her about Nicki. When I was finished and had composed myself, the storekeeper walked over to a floral English armchair with a knitted red throw over one arm. Picking up a paperback book that was resting on a table beside it, she asked, "Have you read this? It's so similar to your story." She handed me the book: *The Shop on Blossom Street*, by Debbie Macomber. The cover showed a storefront with a beautiful window box full of fresh flowers, which looked much like this shop. "Are you familiar with Debbie Macomber?" she asked.

When I told her that I hadn't read the book but that, yes, I was familiar with the author's work, she proceeded to fill me in. "Do you know that Debbie Macomber is a knitter? She has a whole series of books about a yarn shop, and the stories are about the lives of the people who take classes there. I really think you should read this one, because it just sounds so much like your Nicki's story. Tell you what—why don't you take this? Here, it's my gift. Take it."

Because I was in the process of trying to move forward, I declined. "Thank you," I said, "but I'm going to pass. It's very kind of you to offer, but I really don't want to revisit this. I'll look at some yarn, however. Maybe I'll take up knitting again." I smiled as we moved over to the racks.

I purchased some golden alpaca silk yarn and a sweater pattern, thanked her for listening to me and for the offer of the book, then left to go eat lunch. There was a quaint little restaurant just down the street from the yarn shop, so I decided to try it out, and ordered a lobster on a croissant and a glass of Chardonnay. The weather was lovely, and I felt at peace, but suddenly I couldn't get the idea of the book out of my mind. Why had this happened? I believed that everything happens for I reason, but I chose to let it go without pursuing the question.

Later that afternoon, back at the house, I still couldn't stop thinking about it. Did someone else go through what Nicki did? Did it have a happy ending? And why should I care? It was fiction; my daughter was real, and had died. You don't need to be reminded of all the pain, I thought. Keep moving on. You're doing great. But the woman had said it was about a teenaged girl with a malignant brain tumor. If nothing else, it might give me some more perspective into what some of the applicants for the foundation were going through. Not everybody's story was identical to Nicki's. There—that rationale worked! I jumped in the car and drove back to the yarn shop to get the book before the store closed.

Once I started reading, I couldn't put it down. The story of a teenaged girl who found out that she had a malignant brain tumor? The pain? The hospital stays? The chemotherapy? Missing her whole junior year of high school? And the isolation she felt being a teen with cancer? Where did she get this story? Did she hear about Nicki somehow? I had to know! As I read on, though, I realized that there was one big difference: the book's main character survived her brain tumor. I know the whole story, the true one: most people don't survive a brain tumor. So, I thought, what about the rest of the story? I have to write it. People need to know how to survive this kind of pain. I'd kept all of my journals; I *have* to do this.

When I got back home to Florida, I e-mailed Debbie Macomber, because I had to know where she got her story. She responded right away; the book wasn't about Nicki—it was fiction, though she agreed that it was very much like what Nicki had gone through. We e-mailed back and forth for a couple of weeks, talking, and I was thankful that she was so open with me. Then, several months later, I was surprised when I got a postcard in the mail informing me that Debbie would be doing a book signing at our local bookstore. I was even more surprised when Debbie asked me to meet her privately for ice cream before the book signing. There, not only did I get a private audience with Debbie, but I also met Debbie's editor, Paula Eykelhof. We started talking, and I told her about the Nicki Leach Foundation. Paula's publishing company had a grant program for nonprofits, and she suggested that I apply. I was excited to hear about the grant, and agreed to apply, but I knew I would need guidance with the application process, so we arranged to stay in touch.

It was after this encounter with Debbie and Paula that I decided to write Nicki's story. I wanted to unite with other hurting people, and I felt that a book could reach and impact more people of all ages, bringing awareness to these teen and college-age students with cancer but nowhere to go for help. I hoped that by writing Nicki's story, it would help our foundation grow so we won't have to turn so many deserving young adults with cancer away. Having new contacts with people in the literary and publishing industry helped motivate me. And, the fact that I hadn't ever thought I would be happy again after losing Nicki, and now suddenly I was, seemed reason enough to share my story—I could give hope to others and impact their lives in a positive way.

Although I didn't really know anything about writing—except for writing in my journals for most of my life—I thought maybe Paula would help me. And that she did! Meeting Debbie and Paula was such an inspiration for me. I was hurting, and they reached out to me with kindness, encouraging me to write my book. These happy events were gifts from heaven.

At home, after the meeting with Debbie and Paula, I closed my eyes and smiled, thanking Nicki for giving me wings to fly—and especially for always reminding me to follow my heart.

2010

Here we are at the start of a new decade: another new beginning. They say that time heals all wounds, but I don't think that's true; it just softens them a bit. Every day, there are still so many reminders of what I lost when Nicki died, like when I see a four-year-old ballerina in a tutu, or a red Mini Cooper in traffic—Nicki wanted a red Mini Cooper—or any of the other million things out there that remind me of her. I loved her with my whole heart, and Nicki's life and death will always be with me, no matter what year or decade it is. Five years after her passing, at times I still feel a sense of déjà vu, thinking that Nicki should call me or will be coming home soon. It feels like she's just been on a long vacation, or away at school, and it's been too long without her presence. Then reality hits me. But I know that it's only for a little while that I'll ultimately be without her.

I'll always keep Nicki's memory alive and continue to help others like her, but moving forward after losing a child takes a long time. Life is a series of moving ons, though, and I have chosen to deliberately go forward with my life, putting one foot in front of the other. Sometimes I drag my feet when I remember how much I miss her laughter melting my heart, but most days, I walk confidently—even running once in a while.

Today I drove to my daughter's grave to bury the many cards and letters that people sent to our family after her passing. I had stored them under the bed in my guest room, which used to be Jesse's room. The letters and mementos, some with beautiful prayers and poems, filled their purpose in their own time, but I didn't ever want to read them again, because they would make me sad. Knowing the cards and letters were still with me in the house wasn't helping me anymore, and I thought, What if I died? It would be so sad for Jesse to have to deal with them. He might feel like I did: sad if he kept them, but guilty if he threw them away. They were about Nicki, and more importantly, they were about her passing. And she's not here anymore. So why should these cards and letters remain with us? It seemed cruel to throw these away, but they had served their purpose and now were a part of the past. Reading them again would take me back to where I don't want to be. I had been through the dark, lonely forest, and finally I was seeing the sunshine peek through the trees.

So after five years, I realized what I needed to do: to bury them with Nicki's body. I drove to the cemetery, bringing the cardboard box filled with sympathy cards and letters to her grave, and I dug a hole next to her resting place. Then, I buried all of the cards and letters, just like I had buried her. Back then, so many caring friends dearly supported our family in our time of need. Yet now, I knew it was time to be strong and bury the past. Not the memories—those will live on in my heart forever.

When I came home, it felt right knowing that the sympathy cards and letters were now part of the earth, and not in the house any more. The pain and the sadness from her disease were in the past, while I was in the present. Nicki was with God. There is no safer or better place to be, I know that. I now have closure with this matter.

Over the years, I've found that yoga and meditation are good ways to relax and embrace my life. I also do a couple things to feel good that may seem superstitious, though I think they're anything but; I like to do these little rituals because they bring me joy. I'm a spiritual person who believes that everything happens directed by the hand of God. When I follow my heart, I know that He is my heart, so I'm following His direction. Ten years ago, when Jesse was seventeen, I started collecting pennies, at a time in my life when Jesse was heavy on my heart and mind. He was on the road during his summer vacation from high school, traveling with a rock band and playing guitar, with members who were much older that he was, and I worried about him and missed him. I didn't want to let him go because of his age, but his father let him. So as a mother I could only worry about him and ask God to watch over him.

One day while I was at the supermarket, I started to feel unusually anxious. As I was leaving the market and walking through the parking lot to my car, I noticed something on the pavement, reflecting the setting sun with a bright, warm glow. I was curious, and looked down to see what it was. There on the ground was a shiny new penny lying heads-up. After I stooped down to pick it up, I read the inscription: "In God We Trust." Instantly, I felt relieved, and I knew that God was assuring me He was watching over my son. After that day, every time I find a stray penny, I always pick it up, squeeze it in my hand, and thank God. I say a prayer for Jesse, and I'm assured that God is watching over him. I keep these special pennies in my treasure box in my bedroom, as a symbol of protection and reminder to always trust in God.

I also follow another tradition, one that related to Chinese fortunes. Since Nicki loved Chinese food, especially orange chicken, we often ate at Chinese restaurants. After eating, I could always hardly wait until our waiter brought my fortune cookie, with a special message in it just for me. Nicki always laughed at me because I got so excited, and I would make her wait until I opened mine and read it to her before she could open hers. So now, when I'm feeling defeated, I open my little red box where I store my fortunes and read them just to remind myself to keep dreaming and believing, because my dreams just might come true.

Most of all, though, it was the magnificent Atlantic Ocean that became my solace after Nicki's passing. The gentle breeze and rushing waves would calm my mind and helped to heal my wounds. When I walked along the sandy shore, I would pick up shells, and in that way started my collection. So far, I've collected over two hundred of those unique "brain shells" since the mysterious lady on the beach gave me my first one. After our chance encounter, I researched the name of these shells and found that they're actually called Olive shells—making it even more mysterious that the lady on the beach that day called it a brain shell. Why did she do that?

My collection has grown so much over the years that I made a box out of wood, then painted it white and covered the front of it with glass. This is where I display my brain shells; I love them because they're unique and beautiful— just like Nicki was. The collection hangs in my kitchen, and every day when I look at it I'm reminded that Nicki is marking her path for me to follow: a path to freedom and acceptance. I follow every step with trust. Every night, I wish on the brightest star in the sky, and I know it's "Star 17," her lucky number and her lucky star. She never did tell me why seventeen was her lucky number, so when I see her again I'm going to ask her. Now, though, it's her spirit that shines upon me.

Jesse is technically an only child now, but in reality he isn't, and it always makes it hard to answer when someone asks me if I have children. The first year after Nicki died, I always told the truth, that I have two children, but the truth always became too personal for me, and too sad to relive, especially to strangers or people that I'm concerned won't understand. I've found that it usually makes people sad to know that my child died, and of course it makes me sad too. I don't want to make people feel uncomfortable—and besides, Nicki's life is a cherished memory, not to be shared lightly.

So now, when someone asks me if I have children, I feel happy and proud to tell them about Jesse. He is here, with me, and I'm thankful to tell others about him. Jesse has grown so much since Nicki's death, and I hope that he's found ways to embrace happiness. Based on our many heartfelt discussions, I do believe he's happy. By the time he moved back to Jacksonville in 2008, he hadn't played his guitar for several years, and I was so glad when, one day, he chose to play it again. After so long, he wondered why he'd put his guitar down, but I thought it made perfect sense. Nicki was sick for three years, and the grieving period after losing a loved one is long and tedious; it complicates your thinking and makes you question what you want. For example, when Nicki died, I didn't know what I wanted to do with the rest of my life. I was confused after losing her, and it became difficult for me to continue doing the things that I loved—everything that I'd done up to that point included her in some way. After her passing, all my passions became sad reminders of the past, and just made me sad. I stopped listening to music and taking walks, things that I'd loved doing with her, since they just reminded me that she was gone and was never coming back. But as time passed, I realized that I couldn't give up the things that I love, and besides, she wouldn't want me to. So now I embrace them with even more vigor. I'm also more aware of just how short our lives are, now, and want to make every minute count. It's important to be intentional with our actions and with whom we choose to be with in the short time we're given.

Jesse loved playing his guitar, though—I'd seen his intensity and determination from a young age. God had given him so much talent, and I hoped that he would play again, but it had to be his decision. So I never said a word to him about it, waiting for him to decide on his own. I'm so proud of how quickly Jesse has moved forward with his life and the way he follows his own dream, making his living doing what he loves to do: writing, playing guitar, and producing music. He seems to be creating music with even more intensity these days: he teaches, plays in a worship band at church, and even put his own band together, called Juicy Pony. Along with music, he worked hard to become a black belt in Brazilian Jiu-Jitsu! I appreciate him for everything he has accomplished in his life. I'm proud of him, and I'm glad that he can see me happy now; I feel that we finally share an open, honest relationship. What I want most for Jesse is to stay happy, and I will always love him no matter what he chooses to do with his life. It's his decision, and he owes me nothing. I love him unconditionally.

On Easter Sunday, 2008, about three years after Nicki's passing, while standing on the dunes overlooking Nicki's beloved beach during sunrise service, the man I had been dating presented me with a tear-shaped diamond ring. I thought about the teardrop shape, realizing that the ring symbolized the many tears I have cried on my journey to happiness. I wondered why he would give me a ring shaped that way. It's true that I will always carry sadness in my heart, but there will always be a smile on my face. Although I cared for him, losing a child is a very long grieving process, and I couldn't make the life-changing decision to marry again while in mourning. I was so lonely after Nicki died, and it had been so long since I'd been with a man—with a husband. After Mike left, I found that I couldn't bear being alone. I craved companionship, but I knew that I had to come out of grieving before making any lifelong decisions. I wasn't ready yet. I needed to be alone.

These days, I'm not in any hurry to get married again. I still have to grieve my marriage and my husband, as I haven't done that yet. I want to be healthy and strong before I make another commitment to anyone. I also have to find myself, discover who I am. Before Nicki's death I was a wife and the mother of two teenagers. But who am I now? I have to find out, and I want to be able to enjoy my own company for a little longer—I need to get to know this new me. The man I was dating was much older than me, and we both came into our relationship with very recent loses, especially me—having just lost my child to cancer and my marriage less than a year previously. I'm sure that entering into a new relationship wouldn't be smart. I'm still grieving and healing today, and I may never want to marry again. I don't know: time will tell.

I'm very peaceful being alone in my home now, and am thankful for this time to heal. I hold good memories here in this house, on this beach, in this town—too many to leave it just yet. My house and my life are comfortable, and I treasure the fact that this is all mine. I value my own space, and need to be alone to write, which has become my passion. I like my life just the way it is: I'm right where God has placed me.

Most of my time now is devoted to running the foundation and other Nicki-related projects. It took some time, but I had all of Nicki's photographs mounted, framed, and displayed in local art fairs, art walks, and galleries. Some of her photographs hang in professional buildings to raise awareness of the Nicki Leach Foundation. One day, while going through her camera bag, I found a roll of film—still in her camera—and two other undeveloped rolls in her case. I rushed to the photo store as fast as I could, eager to see what she left behind—treasures I knew were sent from heaven above. Once the film was developed, we found more photos of ducks, turtles, and the oleander tree that I had never even seen. Today I have copies of everything displayed in my home, along with her haiku and a portrait of Nicki painted by the artist Ellen Jones, Jesse's former youth teacher at church.

Nicki's spirit continues to be present all around me. I feel her everywhere, especially when I meditate, which I've learned to do frequently. Although I do have a life outside of my house, I prefer to be at home. I still have a passion for long walks on the beach, and I make them a priority. I know that the time Nicki spent on the beach was tranquil, as it is also for me, and I realize that our walks together helped us to relax and enjoy our time together for what it was. I still feel the peace we shared when I spend time reflecting there, surrounded by her spirit and her euphoria.

The holidays will always be difficult for me, but fortunately spring comes early to northeast Florida. I still love April, even though it is the month that took Nicki from us. Instead, April is the month that I tend to Nicki's garden at the cemetery where she was laid to rest. And each fall, I celebrate Nicki's birthday with a big bouquet of roses, while I wait for the ducks and turtles to return to the pond behind my house. To this day, I believe that Nicki sends them to make me smile.

Yes, I've stayed busy these past few years—although I have yet to knit a sweater!—spending time with the people I love, helping those I can, enjoying my independence. And in every spare moment, I write.

HEAVEN

When I was a little girl, living by the railroad tracks in Grass Lake, Michigan, I once wrote a letter to God. When I finished writing, I folded my letter up, closed my eyes, then threw it up in the air, hoping it would go to heaven and God would read it. I know it was kind of silly, because I could have just talked to Him silently and He would have heard me, but I wanted to write God an actual letter. Even as a young girl I loved to write. It is comforting, though, to know that He knows our hearts and what we are thinking, even before we think it. Even before we even pray, He answers us.

Nicki's death changed my life dramatically. I'm not the same person I was when she was here with me; I'm a better person because of her. She still guides me daily and comes to me in so many ways. Recently I visited Montana's Glacier National Park, and, as I rested in a field, a number of butterflies came and perched on my hand, head, arms, and legs. I felt so loved! I was mesmerized by their brilliant, colorful wings, which made me think of angels. I knew Nicki was reminding me about the freedom in my life, and thought about her final wish for happiness to me. I remember asking Nicki, when she was just a wee little girl, what she would wish for if she knew it would be granted. Immediately, she said, "That I could fly." Her wish came true—and she must have shared it with me, because now we can both fly.

Since Nicki doesn't need my prayers anymore, I ask her to pray for me. She's fully aware of what is going on, here on this earth, and I am thankful that her spirit is living within my heart. When I talk to her, I can hear her replies; when I close my eyes, she comes ever so softly, just like a saint, in vision and voice. A warm feeling comes over me, and I feel her embrace. My mind and my soul are entwined with hers. It's hard to let go.

On that special day, April 26, 2005, when Nicki released my hand and went into a coma, she needed my reassurance that I would be all right; she wanted me to release her and let her go, set her free. I was her mommy, and she wanted my permission. It was the hardest thing that I have ever had to do because I never wanted to let her go, but God was not going to give in to me. I knew that then, and I know that now. I've learned to simply trust Him, and never to resist in any way. I'm fortunate that my daughter left me so many things to do with my remaining time on this earth, especially her assignment to help others. She told me not to be sad but rather to smile, to try to stay positive and healthy. She asked me to help other people with cancer, because so many people had loved and helped her throughout her disease. She always took care of me and praised me for being strong, but I wonder if she knew that in fact *she* was my strength.

I remember one morning when I was in my bedroom, getting dressed while listening to the radio. Nicki came in and sat on my bed, as she so often did, stretched out against my headboard with her legs crossed in front of her. My room was filled with the sound of Bette Midler singing; it was "You Are the Wind Beneath My Wings." Nicki sat quietly for a while, listening to the song, and then she looked at me and said, "That's how I feel about you, Mommy." I choked up; I never could handle it when she wanted to be realistic about what was coming—it made me too emotional. So I held back my tears, and just smiled.

Every time I hear that song, now, I start crying because I know that she can fly without my wind: she's flying with her own wings. I hope she knew that she was my strength. Thank you, Nicki, for being my wind and for giving me wings—not only to fly, but because you gave me permission to find joy for the rest of my life. Thank you for your order to "Be happy, Mommy."

I can't help but grieve for my daughter, but it's different when believers grieve. We grieve with hope, because we know we will see our loved ones again. I live and breathe to hold my child in my arms again. I'm now at peace and thankful that Nicki has been rewarded, advanced to heaven and promoted to a new life. She will live forever with God, who loves each and every one of His children. She's waiting for me and Jesse and her dad, and all the people that she loved here on earth. I don't know how long I will live, but I will never fear death. I know that I, too, will one day be held in the arms of Jesus, whose arms are big enough to hold both Nicki and me, along with my dad, my grandparents, and everyone else I love who has gone before me. It is comforting to know that we all have an invitation to live with Him forever. I don't think I could ever be happy again without knowing that.

Sometimes I wonder if Nicki will recognize me when I get to heaven, because I will be much older than when she last saw me. But then I'm reminded that God has these things all worked out for us. I imagine that, right after I stand before Him, I will run into Nicki's arms and hold her forever. She will recognize me, and I will recognize her, no longer sick or in pain, but healthy and beautiful and whole once again. And I will hear her laughter again, too, the laughter that could melt people's hearts, for in the Bible, Luke 6:21 says, "God will bless you people who are crying. You will laugh." I'm also comforted knowing that there will be singing and dancing in heaven, as 1 Chronicles 25:1-8 says that people are praising God with their voices and musical instruments. I'm satisfied knowing where Nicki is, and sometimes imagine what she is doing—and I know that Nicki must be entertaining others in heaven. I can't wait to see the show.

Recently, I love going to Montana to see the mountains, so high and mighty. I know that it takes a strong person to get to the top of mountains so tall. I'm not a mountain climber, but I would love to see the view from the top. At times I wonder if I'll make it, but one thing is for sure: I will never stop trying to make it to the top. I'm just a short time away from Nicki as I write this, and finally I know that I am all right. Being all right is honoring what Nicki wanted for me, and what God has placed before me—this journey that I call living beyond myself. This world is cruel, harsh, hard, violent, and dangerous. There is beauty all around, but there is also so much suffering. We need God. I will never take the chance of not seeing my baby again by not believing.

Something I notice now is mothers and daughters everywhere, especially at the mall. At times, it seems like the world is full of only mothers and daughters! I often watch them having lunch together, which I've missed so much since my daughter's been gone. I want to stop them and tell them how blessed they are. I want to show Nicki's picture to them, and smile when they remark at how beautiful she is, and that I must miss her a lot. Then I want to tell them how we used to do exactly what they're doing. I want to follow them around, join them, and be a part of what they have—what I lost.

But instead I embrace my freedom and independence and simply keep smiling. I keep holding onto memories of Nicki, and she keeps guiding me as I continue to move forward each day. I've tried to put into words the ache and the loneliness that I carry inside me, but now I'm thankful that there is more joy than pain. Nicki's smile and the sound of her voice are the things that will stay with me, playing over and over in my mind. On and on it goes: missing, longing, waiting—but also rejoicing.

God has filled me with love, and over the years I've changed. I've learned to be strong and to stand for what I believe in. Nicki convinced me to always follow my heart. I know my daughter was smiling from heaven when she heard Ryan repeat those words at her funeral: "Don't frown because it's over... smile because it happened." In fact, I believe that Nicki knew her life would be short. When she found out that she had a stage-four malignant brain tumor, she said, "I always wondered what my thing would be." Could she have known about the legacy she would eventually leave for others who are suffering from cancer?

The day after Nicki died, I turned to Jesse with tears in my eyes and said, "I'm not sure if I'm still Nicki's mommy." I was so confused. But he reassured me as he always has when he looked at me with compassion and answered,

"You will always be Nicki's mommy." I've come a long way since that day years ago; now, I'm assured that Nicki is at peace and in heaven. As I promised her, I'm all right.

She is just around the corner from our earthly realm— and yet so near that I can still feel the warmth of her smile in my heart every day.

God didn't answer my prayer to keep my daughter on this earth. I don't know why. I'm sad about that, but I still trust God and love Him, and I know that it's His promise that one day I will see my sweet baby girl again. This I know for sure. So I follow her lead, and I don't frown because it's over. It's not over. I smile because it happened. I smile because my Nicki lives on in the lives of those she continues to bless through her foundation. I smile because Nicki is still smiling.

ACKNOWLEDGMENTS

God, thank you for always providing for me, especially during my greatest times of need. You held my hands through the writing of my memoir, guiding me throughout my journey. You are the love of my life.

This book would not have been possible without the following people:

My mom, Beverly Coleman-Warren I love you immensely, forever and into eternity. You have always been such a great mom to me. And to Marv Warren.

To my best friend, and the nicest person I have ever known: my sister Lynn.

And my brother Kenneth, a kind generous soul, who paints with passion.

To my nieces Justina and Dawn: I love you, sweet, beautiful girls.

I realize I have not always been readily available throughout the years, but my love for my family cannot be measured by time or distance. My love is real and is always there.

To Paula Eykelof, a very special lady and editor who helped me an incredible amount with this book. Paula is the executive editor at Harlequin Publishing, and has worked with writer—and my friend—Debbie Macomber for over twenty-five years. I first met Paula in Jacksonville, FL, when she was traveling with Debbie Macomber during her book-signing tour; Debbie was gracious enough to call me and ask to meet with her and Paula before her book signing. After that meeting, through a series of e-mails that went back and forth for over four years, Paula tutored me and encouraged my work while I wrote this story. Thank you, Paula, for your kindness and generosity. And thank you, Debbie, for writing *The Shop on Blossom Street*, the book that inspired me to tell Nicki's story.

My special friend Lorrie Barry: who walked beside me when my daughter was diagnosed with a malignant brain tumor. You saw the devastation that I went through, and never left my side. After Nicki's passing, you encouraged me to write a book, truly believing that telling Nicki's story would help others overcome loss and hardships in their own lives. You kept me focused through the difficult stuff, like recalling timelines, events, and dates that were still so painful—things that I had pushed away to the back of my mind. Lorrie, you exemplify what true friendship is.

Terri Devall, my lifelong friend, who I will always think of as my other sister: thank you for designing our logo for the Nicki Leach Foundation, as well as our brochures, business cards, posters and helping with the foundation. I value our friendship more every year, and I'm thankful that we have remained close for over forty years. Our love will last a lifetime.

Priscilla Johnson: I grew to love you through your love for Nicki. I am fortunate to call you my friend. I'm sure that each and every mother would love to have a woman like you to mentor their daughter, the way you did my daughter Nicki. Thank you for all the times you have come to my rescue, and encouraged me through difficult days.

Ellen Jones: thank you for painting Nicki's portrait, and for capturing her grace and elegance on canvas. Thank you for your donations to the Nicki Leach Foundation to help our young adults with cancer.

Heather Nickodem, Nicki's fifth grade teacher. When I

found out that she had retired from teaching to become a writer, I called her and asked if she would help me with my manuscript, as I had never written a book. Heather became more than just a helpmate during the months that she worked beside me: she became my friend. Thank you, Heather, for helping to bring Nicki's spirit alive through words.

Susan Brandenburg came into my life in 2006 when I was creating the website for the Nicki Leach Foundation. She amazes me with the way she can make words come alive with emotion and color. Thank you, Susan, for adding your final touch to my story—but most of all thank you for feeling my daughter's spirit.

Alex Dougherty, Nicki's friend and fellow classmate from Douglas Anderson School of the Arts: thank you for writing the song "Nicolette" to express how the death of someone special in your life can affect you. Thank you for letting us know how important she is and always will be, in your life and others' lives as well. May she forever meet you in your dreams.

I also want to thank my community for their loving support of our family during Nicki's illness. Nicki felt loved and cared for through your delicious meals and the many cards and gifts that you gave her. Your kindness will always be remembered.

CREDITS

Scripture: *The Learning Bible,* Contemporary English Version

"The Voice Within," Christina Aguilera

"Alfie," Burt Bacharach and Hal David

Nicki Leach Foundation logo: Terri Devall-Devall Design, Ltd., www.Terridevalldesign.com

Susan the Scribe, Inc., Susanscribe@comcast.net

Oil Portraits: Original Sacred Artwork by Ellen Jones, www.Joypeace3art.com

Ten percent of all portrait commissions go to the Nicki Leach Foundation

Nicki Leach

FOUNDATION

"Don't frown because it's over…
smile because it happened."

www.nickileach.org

Helping Young Adults with Cancer

We provide modest scholarships for their education to young adults (age 15–39) who have cancer, and we support glioblastoma research in young adult tumors.

ABOUT ATMOSPHERE PRESS

Atmosphere Press is an independent full-service publisher for books in genres ranging from non-fiction to fiction to poetry, with a special emphasis on being an author-friendly approach to the challenges of getting a book into the world. Learn more about what we do at atmospherepress.com.

We encourage you to check out some of Atmosphere's latest releases, which are available at Amazon.com, BarnesandNoble.com, and via order from your local bookstore:

Let the Little Birds Sing, a novel by Sandra Fox Murphy

Leaving the Ladder, nonfiction by Lynda Bayada

They Are Almost Invisible, poems by Elizabeth Carmer

Spots Before Stripes, a YA novel by Jonathan Kumar

Owlfred the Owl Learns to Fly, a picture book
    by Caleb Foster

Mandated Happiness, a novel by Clayton Tucker

Transcendence, poems and images by Vincent Bahar Towliat

Love Your Vibe, nonfiction by Matt Omo

Time Do Not Stop, poems by William Guest

Bello the Cello, a picture book by Dennis Mathew

That Scarlett Bacon, a picture book by Mark Johnson

Makani and the Tiki Mikis, a picture book by Kosta Gregory

Adrift, poems by Kristy Peloquin

Dear Old Dogs, a novella by Gwen Head

Ghost Sentence, poems by Mary Flanagan

What Outlives Us, poems by Larry Levy

How Not to Sell, nonfiction by Rashad Daoudi

That Beautiful Season, a novel by Sandra Fox Murphy

What I Cannot Abandon, poems by William Guest

All the Dead Are Holy, poems by Larry Levy

Rescripting the Workplace, nonfiction by Pam Boyd

ABOUT BUNNY LEACH

Bunny Leach's background is rich in variety, giving her a distinct authorial advantage in creating the heart-wrenching and reflective memoir and self-help book *Letting Nicki Go*. Seamlessly blending her history and experiences during her daughter's battle with cancer with keen introspective meditations on faith and lessons about grief and healing, Leach uses her life story with wit and grace to offer the reader a redemptive experience of their own.

Born in Michigan, Bunny left the state after an early marriage to her first husband, a rising star on the Association of Tennis Professionals ATP tour, traveling widely and living abroad with her spouse and subsequently their two small children. Bunny developed her observational skills as a temporary ex-pat and young mother, as well as the start of a journaling habit that would serve her well throughout the years. Upon returning to the States, the family settled in Florida, where Bunny took on full-time responsibilities as a homemaker and mother, diving into community life and using her spare time to further her interests in writing and home design.

After her teenage daughter's death from cancer, Bunny returned to college at the University of North Florida and, after studying a course direction in psychology, she became a certified life coach helping people find the answers that lie within themselves so that they may achieve their dreams and goals. Additionally, after a successful one-woman renovation of her beloved beach home in Florida, Bunny began work in home staging and redesign, and is pleased to offer her services to individuals and realtors alike.

Before her daughter died, Nicki asked her mother if she would do something to help others who are suffering with cancer like she was. In Nicki's memory Bunny began the Nicki Leach Foundation, a non-profit organization providing education scholarships and funding for cancer research on AYA tumors (Adolescence and Young Adults), age 15-39. As the founder and CEO of the foundation, Bunny plays an integral role in ensuring that her daughter's memory is kept alive through constant generosity and meaningful action, providing the material means to further the dreams and goals of other young people afflicted with cancer.

Bunny also began volunteering her time and efforts as a Patient Advocate working with the American Society of Clinical Oncology ASCO.org, and is a member of the Molecular Tumor board for TAPUR, the Targeted Agent Profiling Utilization Registry (tapur.org). She is on the patient advocate committee for the Alliance (alliance forclinicaltrialsinoncology.org), which is supported by the NCI National Cancer Institute.

Bunny lives in Ponte Vedra Beach, Florida with her husband, enjoying the beauty of the ocean and her daily walks and meditation, which is so important for her. She is writing a new nonfiction book, *Mourning Mothers*, and a novel, *Once A Week*. The follow-up to *Letting Nicki Go*, called *Breathing New Life: Finding Happiness after Tragedy*, is also available from Atmosphere Press and can be purchased online.

Nicki, Thanksgiving 2004, five months
Before she died